WILLIAM BARCLAY

The Lord's Supper

D0770311

SCM PRESS LTD

To the Memory of
Thomas Marshall
once minister of
Dalziel North Church, Motherwell,
who prepared me
for my first Communion

334 00932 4

First published 1967
by SCM Press Ltd
58 Bloomsbury Street, London WC1
Fifth impression 1978

Printed in Great Britain by
Lewis Reprints Ltd
member of Brown Knight & Truscott Group
London and Tonbridge

CONTENTS

FOREWORD

IN the nature of things no one will ever write a book about the sacrament of the Lord's Supper with which everyone will agree. I am grateful for the opportunity to write this book, but I am also conscious that it is one man's view. I know well that there are many to whom the sacrament is the most precious thing on earth. But I also know well that there are many more to whom the sacrament means nothing but an ununderstood conventional act of traditional piety. After thirteen years in the parish ministry and twenty years' university teaching I have come to the conclusion that, when we can neither grasp nor teach the whole truth, it is better to get hold of some part of the truth which we can understand, and on which we can act. I have not myself a mind trained either in philosophy or in theology, and all I have tried to do is to examine the history of the sacrament, and then to set down a view of it which I know is incomplete and which has yet been very precious to myself and which I know means something vital to those to whom it has been throughout the years presented. I shall be more than satisfied if I can succeed in making some people not so much understand as think it out for themselves.

I owe many debts to many books, but I must set down my special debt to the magnificent article on the Eucharist in Hastings' *Encyclopaedia of Religion and Ethics*. That article does not seek to explain or construct, but historically it is invaluable.

I have to thank the Rev. John Bowden, the editor of the SCM Press, for first of all allowing me to write this book, and for his patience and encouragement when it was being written.

The University of Glasgow   WILLIAM BARCLAY
June 1967

1

THE NECESSITY TO UNDERSTAND

In his posthumous volume *The Theology of the Sacraments*, Donald Baillie quotes a saying of Tillich to the effect that we are living in an age of the Church in which we are threatened with 'the death of the sacraments'.[1] This may well be so. Even if the sacraments are celebrated as often as ever, it may still be true that they are becoming stranger and stranger, and less and less meaningful to those who share in them. The sacraments are still built into the structure of the Church, but for many they have become a ritual rather than a reality. There are certain reasons for this.

There is one sense of the word sacrament which is easy to follow and to understand. The Latin word *sacramentum* has a curious history. It began by meaning the sum which two contending parties deposited in court when they entered upon a law-suit. In the early days the sum was in sheep or oxen. The successful party received his deposit back, but the loser forfeited his, and the forfeited pledge was often used for religious purposes – hence the name *sacramentum*, the sacred thing. Here, then, the meaning is a pledge.

But this word *pledge* has another sense; it can mean a promise, and that is what *sacramentum* moves on to mean. And it was one particular pledge. It was the military oath of allegiance which a soldier took when he joined the Roman army.[2] It was administered in a dramatic way. The tribune himself, the regimental commander, took it first. He then

[1] Donald Baillie, *The Theology of the Sacraments*, p. 39; Paul Tillich, *The Protestant Era*, p. 48.
[2] Tacitus, *Annals* I.28.

assembled his regiment. One man was picked out. This man
repeated the pledge in full, and swore that he would obey the
commands of his general and that he would execute them to the
best of his ability, that he would always meet at the commands
of the consul, and that he would never leave the regimental
standards and flee from the field of battle. The rest of the
regiment came forward, and one by one each man said: 'The
same for me.'[3] In addition to being a pledge of loyalty, this
promise gave the soldier the right to fight. It was only the man
who had taken the oath who could go to war without being
guilty of murder and rapine. Further, the oath was taken with
a curse called down on the man who broke it, and therefore,
if a soldier did break his oath of loyalty, his general could
execute him on the spot without further trial. In an emergency,
when there was no time to go through the formal taking of the
oath individually, the commander simply said: 'Let those who
desire the safety of the Republic follow me!' And a united shout
of response was taken as a pledge.[4] By this oath the soldiers
swore that to them the safety of the Emperor was the most
important thing in life, and that they held him dearer than
themselves and their children.[5] For the Roman soldier the
sacramentum was the declaration of a loyalty than which none
could be more far-reaching.

The word further expanded. In imperial times it became the
custom for loyal citizens voluntarily to take the *sacramentum*
to the Emperor, and to renew it on the anniversary each year of
the day on which they had taken it.[6] In the end *sacramentum*
came to stand for any obligation solemnly taken, as when
Horace declares that he has given no faithless *sacramentum*.[7]
From beginning to end a *sacramentum* means a complete and
solemn promise of complete and absolute and, if need be,
sacrificial loyalty.

If we approach the word sacrament on these lines there is
no difficulty about its meaning. It may not be the main meaning
of the word as it is now used, but it must never be forgotten

---

[3] Polybius, 6.21.2; Livy, 22.38.   [4] Donatus on Terence's *Eunuch*, 4.7.2.
[5] Suetonius, *Caligula* 15.   [6] Tacitus, *Annals* I.7,8; Pliny, *To Trajan* 52.
[7] Horace, *Odes* 2.17.10.

that that meaning is there. To join with Christ's people in the sacrament, and to take the bread and wine in our hands and on our lips is a pledge of absolute loyalty to Jesus Christ.

But this is not the commonest meaning that the word *sacramentum* has in the Christian Church. Augustine defined the word *sacramentum*. 'Signs', he wrote, 'when they are connected with divine things are called sacraments.'[8] A sign, *signum* in Latin, *sēmeion* in Greek, is something which reveals some truth beyond itself. The miracles of Jesus, for instance, are signs, because they reveal something of the nature and the character of the person who does them. A sacrament, then, in this sense will be something, usually a common thing, which has a meaning which is beyond itself.

There is nothing either particularly mysterious or particularly theological about this; it is in fact something which is built into life. We often keep things which are in themselves quite useless, things which to the outsider seem junk, things which some day either we ourselves or someone else will have to throw away. And yet we cannot bear to part with them, because these things have associations and awaken memories and have a meaning far beyond themselves. I have a great many books, thousands of them; but one of them is dearer to me than any other. It is a little paper-covered volume, getting on for forty years old. If I lost it, I could buy another copy for a few shillings. But on it, in now fading ink, it has written on the fly leaf: 'From W. M. M. to W. B. with grateful regard'. W. M. M. is William Malcolm Macgregor, who taught me all I know about the New Testament and who was the princeliest soul I ever met; W. B. is myself. He gave me the book while I was still a student, for some trifling service that I had been able to render him. If I lost my copy, does anyone think that any other copy of the book would be quite the same to me? The other copy would be the same book with the same contents. But the book with the faded writing has something beyond itself. And that is precisely what a sacrament is. In a sacrament we perform a quite common action, we take in our hands and on our lips quite common things, and yet these ordinary things of

[8] Augustine, *Letters* 138.

time reach out far beyond themselves to eternity. If then this sacramental element runs through all life, why is it that there is any danger of the death of the sacraments?

1. Sacrament and instruction must go hand in hand. It is often held that a sacramental form of worship is better for simple people than a form of worship in which preaching predominates. It is claimed that the sacrament with its pictorial presentation of the truth, and with its dramatic re-enacting of the truth, is better for the simple mind than the comparative intellectualism of preaching. This is very much of a half-truth. The sacrament only becomes effective when it has been preceded by the fullest and the most careful instruction.

A sacrament is a mystery, a *mustērion*, in the New Testament sense of the term. In the New Testament sense of the term a mystery is not something complicated and complex and hard to understand, as it is in the modern sense of the term. A mystery is something, usually in itself quite simple, which is completely obscure to the outsider, but completely meaningful to the initiate. To the uninstructed it is meaningless; to the instructed it is the vehicle of truth and grace. So the action of the Lord's Supper, in which the communicant eats a little piece of bread and swallows a sip of wine often seems to the outsider – for instance, to a child – incomprehensible, or even silly or amusing, while to the believer it is one of the supreme experiences of the Christian life.

We are therefore compelled to the conclusion that sacrament and instruction cannot be separated. The early Church knew this. In *The Treatise on the Apostolic Tradition* of Hippolytus in the seventeenth regulation it is laid down: 'Let a catechumen be instructed for three years.'[9] In the *Pilgrimage* of Egeria, Egeria the Spanish nun describes the services she saw in Jerusalem towards the end of the fourth century. With the catechumens the bishop for forty days went through the whole of Scripture, 'explaining them first literally, and then unfolding them spiritually. He will also teach them about the Resurrection and about all things concerning the faith during this period.' 'The candidates are taught for three hours a day for seven

[9] Cf. the edition of the *Tradition* by Gregory Dix, vol. I, p. 28.

weeks, excluding Saturdays and Sundays.'[10] There was lengthy and detailed instruction prior to baptism, which was the preliminary to the Lord's Supper.

Without instruction to precede it, the Lord's Supper degenerates into either formalism or superstition. A teaching ministry and a sacramental ministry must go hand in hand. It may well be true to say that the greatest failure of the present-day Church lies in its failure to exercise a teaching ministry, and, where there is failure in teaching, there must also be devaluation of the sacraments.

2. There is no doubt that the sacraments are much stranger to the twentieth century than they were to the first. There was scarcely anyone in the ancient world who did not know what a sacramental meal was. The Jews had the Passover as the very centre of their faith, and still have. The Greeks had their Mystery Religions. The Mystery Religions were nearly all founded on passion plays. They were based on the story of some god who had lived and died and who had been resurrected, never to die any more. The story of this god was acted out in a passion play. The worshipper was only allowed to see it after a long course of instruction, and a long period of asceticism. He was shown it under the most deliberately designed emotional conditions, with incense burning and lighting cunningly adjusted and emotive music and a wonderful liturgy. In that experience he was meant to achieve such a unity with the god that he too shared in the god's sufferings and death and in the end in his immortal and undefeatable life. He was supposed to achieve such identity with the god that he could say: 'I am thou, and thou art I.' It was in this pictorial sacramental way that they sought what Evelyn Underhill called 'a veritable access to Ultimates'.[11] They had their baptisms in which the initiate was immersed in water and emerged to be fed with milk like a little child. They had their common meals of bread and wine in which they were the guests of the god. S. Angus says of the Hellenistic Greek of New Testament times: 'Truth came to him in images rather than in ideas; it was symbolic rather

[10] Cf. J. G. Davies, *The Social Life of Early Christians*, pp. 103, 106.
[11] Evelyn Underhill, *Man and the Supernatural*, p. 183.

than dialectic . . . . This mental outlook was more accordant
to a religion in mimetic action than to an exact theology.'[12]

The result of all this was that the ancient world was saturated
in sacrament. Dean Inge said that if Christ had not instituted
baptism and the Eucharist, 'the Church would have had to
invent them. 'A Christianity without sacraments could never
have converted Europe.'[13]

The point of all this is that in the first century there was
nothing more universal than sacramental action; in the
twentieth century there is no such familiarity. In the first
century sacraments could be familiarly accepted; in the twentieth century they have to be laboriously explained. S. Angus
comments on this situation: 'In every religion practices are
more tenacious than beliefs . . . . Cult forms are even more
static than dogmas.' He then goes on to quote Sir James G.
Fraser, who writes: 'The history of religion is a long attempt to
reconcile old custom with new reason, and to find a sound
theory for absurd practices.'[14] We need not necessarily go as
far as that, but we must in trying to understand the Lord's
Supper remember that it was instituted in an age in which it
required little explanation, while we celebrate it in an age
when it is as antiquarian rite, not intelligible without much
explanation.

3. The Lord's Supper runs into another difficulty. At this
stage we can only state this difficulty; we will later have to
try to find some solution to it. The difficulty is this. Into the
Church there came an increasingly literalistic interpretation of
the words of the institution. The bread and the wine were taken
to be more and more literally and physically the body and the
blood of Jesus Christ. This involved what can only be called a
magical change in them. In the early centuries this was an idea
which was easy for an age that was steeped in magical ideas.
In the Middle Ages this line of thought was solidified into a
dogma. With the dawn of modern thought there necessarily

[12] S. Angus, *The Religious Quests of the Graeco-Roman World*, pp. 136 f.
[13] W. R. Inge, *Contentio Veritatis*, p. 279, in S. Angus, *The Religious
Quests of the Graeco-Roman World*, p. 128.
[14] S. Angus, *op. cit.*, p. 131.

came a reaction against this whole area of magical thinking. In wide areas of the Christian Church the idea that the bread and the wine literally become the flesh and the blood of Jesus Christ had to be abandoned. But when it is abandoned, what is to be put in its place? There is a simplicity in the magical idea; it is easily stated; other ideas are far more complicated, and far less easy to state. And the result is that modern man, who is in any event impatient of what he regards as the subtleties of theologians, has become less and less sure of what the Lord's Supper is and of what he is doing when he shares in it.

When Justin Martyr speaks of the Lord's Supper[15] he says: 'This food is called by us the Eucharist'. He then goes on to say that the Eucharist becomes the body and the blood of Christ, 'through the prayer of the word which came from him'. Irenaeus can talk of the blood of Jesus Christ 'from which he moistens our blood . . . and the material bread which he affirmed to be his own body from which he causes our bodies to grow'.[16]

The sheerly magical and physical side of this keeps growing. Tertullian can speak of handling the body of Christ.[17] There is a growing anxiety that not a crumb of the bread or a drop of the wine should fall or be lost.[18] The *Apostolic Tradition* has the same care: 'Let all take care that no unbaptized person taste of the Eucharist, nor a mouse or other animal, and that none of it at all fall and be lost. For it is the Body of Christ to be eaten by them that believe and not to be thought lightly of.' Similarly it is said of the cup: 'Spill not from it, that no alien spirit lick it up.'[19] In the time of Cyprian, the elements have acquired magical powers. A woman secretly partook of the elements and received 'not food but a sword', and was torn with internal convulsions. Another woman tried with unclean hands to open the box where the holy bread was kept, and fire broke out and made it impossible for her to touch it. A man shared in the sacrament unworthily, and, when he received the

---

[15] Justin Martyr, *Apology* I.66.   [16] Irenaeus, *Against Heresies* 5.2,3.
[17] Tertullian, *De Corona* 3.   [18] Origen, *Homily on Exodus* 12.3.
[19] Hippolytus, *The Apostolic Tradition* 32.2–4; cf. *The Canons of Hippolytus* 209.

bread from the priest, it turned to cinders in his hand.[20] Chrysostom can speak of 'burying the teeth in his flesh'.[21] Cyril of Jerusalem begins to use the words 'transformed', 'converted', 'changed', 'altered' of the elements, the change happening as a result of the prayer of consecration.[22] And in the work *Concerning the Mysteries*, attributed to Ambrose of Milan, this is said to happen *praeter naturam*, beyond nature, and the nature of the elements is said to be changed.[23] This comes into the liturgies in such phrases as 'the bread changed into the flesh . . . the cup changed into the blood', 'unto the transformation of the body and blood of our Lord God Jesus Christ', 'to eat the body . . . to drink the blood'.[24]

This kind of thought with its sacramental magic and its literalism bit deep into Christian thought, and in parts of the Church still remains. For perhaps still more, this kind of thought is no longer possible. When it is not possible the question immediately arises, What is to be put in its place? What has to be put in its place is much less apparently simple. There therefore arises a certain vagueness as to the meaning of the Lord's Supper, and therefore less devotion to it.

4. There remains one other reason why the position of the sacrament of the Lord's Supper is difficult today. At least in Protestant thought, the efficacy of a sacrament is allied to the faith which the participant brings to it. There is a sense in which he will get in proportion as he brings. But this is not an age of faith; it is an age of questioning. In the Protestant faith, the sacrament of the Lord's Supper is not so much a begetter of faith as it is a nourisher of faith. It has been called 'the pilgrim hospice', the place into which the traveller on the way turns for strength for the way. From the beginning, by its very nature the sacrament of the Lord's Supper has been for the mature Christian, or at least for the pledged Christian, rather than for the enquirer. But the twentieth century is the age of enquiry rather than of conviction, and of interest rather than

[20] Cyprian, *Concerning the Lapsed* 25, 26.
[21] Chrysostom, *Homily on John* 47.
[22] Cyril of Jerusalem, *Catechetical Lectures* 5.7.
[23] Ambrose, *Concerning the Mysteries* 9.52–54.
[24] J. Hastings, *Encyclopaedia of Religion and Ethics* 5.554.

commitment. There are therefore fewer today who can bring to the sacrament what the sacrament demands.

It is, then, clear from our examination of the situation that an enquiry into the meaning of the Lord's Supper is something which in the present situation is more than worth while.

2

THE PROBLEM OF DATE

WHEN we begin to study the Lord's Supper, we are faced with an astonishing paradox. Without question and without debate, the Lord's Supper is the central action in Christian worship, and yet at the same time there is nothing about it which is certain. There is no way of approaching it without encountering some problems. There are three great problems:

1 What was the original meal?

2 What are the words of the institution?

3 What is the meaning of these words, and what for us is the Lord's Supper meant to be?

To these problems we must address ourselves, and we begin with the problem of what the original meal was.

To put it briefly – was the Last Supper a Passover Meal, or was it not? Or, to put the same question in a different form, are we to accept the account of it in the Synoptic Gospels, or are we to accept the account of it in John?

In this matter there is a curious and a baffling ambiguity in even the simplest statements. In Luke's account[1] Jesus says:

I have earnestly desired to eat this passover with you before I suffer; for I tell you I shall not eat it (or, I shall never eat it again) until it is fulfilled in the kingdom of God.

Is Jesus saying: 'I have earnestly desired to eat this passover with you before I suffer – and my dearest wish has been granted'? Or, is Jesus saying: 'I have earnestly desired to eat

[1] Luke 22.15.

this passover with you before I suffer – but alas it is not to be'? Even in the apparently simple narrative of the Synoptics the questions arise. But let us cite the evidence as it is.

The narrative of the Synoptic Gospels can be summarized as follows. The disciples ask where Jesus intends the Passover preparations to be made. Two of them, named in Luke as Peter and John, are sent on ahead to make the preparations. Clearly, arrangements have been made. They are told that they will see a man carrying a jar of water, and that they are to follow him. To fetch water from the well was distinctively a woman's duty, and any man carrying a jar of water would stand out as a very unusual sight. This is certainly a prearranged code and signal. They are to follow this man. They are to say to the householder of the house into which he goes that the Teacher is asking for the guest room where he is to eat the Passover with his disciples. They will be shown a large upper room ready for them. This they do, and find everything exactly as Jesus had said. There they prepare the Passover, and then the next section of the narrative goes on to say that in the evening Jesus came with the Twelve, and the meal proceeds.[2]

There seems no doubt at all that in that narrative the meal is a Passover meal. But then, strangely enough, there emerges a problem. All three Gospel writers introduce the narrative slightly differently.[3] Matthew has:

Now on the first day of Unleavened Bread . . .

Luke has:

Then came the day of Unleavened Bread, on which the passover lamb had to be sacrificed . . .

Mark has:

And on the first day of Unleavened Bread, when they sacrificed the passover lamb . . .

There is no doubt that in the official Jewish regulations the Festival of Unleavened Bread began *after* the Passover itself was finished. The rule is clear:

[2] Mark 14.12–17; Matthew 26.17–20; Luke 22.7–14.
[3] Mark 14.12; Matthew 26.17; Luke 22.7.

B

In the first month, on the fourteenth day of the month in the evening, is the Lord's passover. And on the fifteenth day of the same month is the feast of unleavened bread to the Lord.[4]

On the fourteenth day of the first month is the Lord's passover. And on the fifteenth day of this month is a feast; seven days shall unleavened bread be eaten.[5]

The matter of dating is further complicated by the fact that in New Testament times the Jewish day begins at 6 p.m. on the previous day. That is to say, for the Jew Friday began at 6 p.m. on Thursday. Therefore, when we would say that the Passover took place on Thursday evening, the Jew would say that it took place on Friday.

To this must be added the fact that the Passover lamb had to be sacrificed before it was eaten at the feast. It was not simply bought and taken home and cooked and eaten. It was bought; it was taken to the Temple to be slain by the priests; the blood of it was drained away, and offered to God, for the blood is the life and belongs only to God. Only then could it be taken away and prepared for the meal. The ceremony of the killing of the lambs began at twelve o'clock midday on the day on the evening of which the Passover was kept, for the Passover had be eaten between 6 p.m. and midnight.

If we tabulate this according to the time-table of the Synoptic Gospels, we get this sequence:

1. Thursday afternoon: the sacrificing of the lambs.

2. Thursday evening (for the Jew, Friday) between 6 p.m. and midnight: the Passover meal.

3. Friday morning: the Festival of Unleavened Bread begins and lasts for the next week.

When, with this time-table in mind, we return to Mark, the contradiction is obvious. Mark says:

On the first day of Unleavened Bread, on which the passover lamb had to be sacrificed,

and Matthew and Luke both speak of the first day, or the day,

---

[4] Leviticus 23.5 f.　　[5] Numbers 28.16 f.

of Unleavened Bread.[6] Quite clearly, the difficulty is that the day when the Passover lamb was sacrificed was not in fact the first day of Unleavened Bread, for the lamb was sacrificed on the Thursday afternoon, and the Festival of Unleavened Bread did not begin until the Friday morning, after the Passover.

What are we to say? Is there here even in the Synoptics the trace of a tradition that the crucifixion did not take place until after the Passover, as in John's tradition? Or, is there some simpler explanation?

Jeremias states as a principle that, when two parallel datings are given, or when two parallel statements are made, the second is always intended to be an explanation of the first.[7] In that case, Mark's primary date is the first day of Unleavened Bread. Does that then absolutely necessitate moving the whole narrative to after the Passover? Not necessarily. There could be a simple mistranslation of an Aramaic phrase, and it could be that what it should mean is: 'On the day before the Feast of Unleavened Bread, on which the Passover lamb had to be sacrificed.'[8] Even more likely, there is simply a looseness of dating. Part of the Passover ritual was that on the Thursday morning there was throughout every house a ceremonial search for leaven. By midday every particle of leaven had to be cleared out of the house, and by 6 p.m. on the evening of the day no leaven could be used for any purpose or for any food. This was because leaven is fermented dough, and the Jews identified fermentation with putrefaction. Leaven was therefore the symbol of evil, and to clear out the leaven was symbolically to eradicate all evil.[9] It would therefore be entirely natural to speak of the day when the leaven was totally banished from the house as the first day of Unleavened Bread, although technically that festival did not begin until the day after.

[6] Mark 14.12; Matthew 26.17; Luke 22.7.
[7] J. Jeremias, *The Eucharistic Words of Jesus*, p. 17. Cf. Mark 1.32.
[8] There would be little change in the Greek. Mark as it stands is: *tē prōtē hēmera tōn azumōn*. The correct version would be: *pro tēs prōtēs hēmeras tōn azumōn*.
[9] For leaven as the symbol of evil, cf. Matthew 16.6, 12; Mark 8.15; Luke 12.1; I Corinthians 5.6; Galatians 5.9.

In spite of some slight doubts, it is fair to take it that the Synoptic writers regard the Last Supper as a Passover meal.

In the Fourth Gospel, whatever problems may arise in regard to its relationship to the Synoptic Gospels, there is no question that it dates the trial and crucifixion of Jesus before the Passover. In it the last meal takes place before the Passover.[10] The Jewish leaders will not enter Pilate's judgment hall,

so that they might not be defiled, but might eat the Passover.[11]

Clearly, they had not yet eaten the Passover, and their fear was that they might be disqualified from doing so. Twice in so many words the Fourth Gospel says that the events of the trial and the crucifixion took place on the day of Preparation of the Passover. When Pilate took his place on his judgment seat, it is said:

Now it was the day of Preparation for the Passover.[12]

The reason for hastening the death of the crucified victims was that it was the day of Preparation.[13]

The Fourth Gospel leaves us in no doubt that it regards the trial and death of Jesus as taking place before the Passover, and that, therefore, the last meal cannot have been a Passover meal, although as we shall see there have been attempts to modify this latter conclusion.

We have, then, to decide whether or not the last meal was a Passover meal, as it is in the Synoptic Gospels, or if it was something else, as it is in the Fourth Gospel, always remembering that in each case there suddenly appear hints which seem to imply the position of the other.

It will help if we outline the Passover ritual, so that we may see if the last meal fits into it. There were six things necessary for the Passover and which had to be prepared in advance.

1. There was the lamb to remind them of the lamb with whose blood the lintel and the door posts of their houses in Egypt had been smeared, so that the angel of death would pass over them in the night of the slaying of the Egyptian first born (Exodus 12.21–23). It had to be cooked in a special way. It must not be boiled or stewed; nothing must touch it, not even

[10] John 13.1 f.   [11] John 18.28.   [12] John 19.14.   [13] John 19.31.

water, not even the sides of a pot. It had to be fixed on a spit which went through it from mouth to vent, and then roasted, entire with head and legs and tail, over an open fire. The minimum number who could constitute a Passover company was twelve, and the lamb had to be eaten entire and nothing left.

2. There was the unleavened bread. Unleavened bread is not like bread at all, but like a water biscuit. It was unleavened bread that the Israelites made on the night of their escape, because there was not time to make leavened bread in the haste of their way-going (Exodus 12.33 f.).

3. There was a bowl of salt water, partly to remind them of the tears they had shed in their wretchedness in Egypt, and partly to remind them of the waters of the Red Sea, through which they had been brought in miraculous safety.

4. There was a collection of bitter herbs, such as horse-radish, chicory, endive, lettuce, horehound, once again to remind them of the bitterness they had endured as slaves. All through this meal there runs the observance of the more than once repeated saying of God to the people: 'You shall remember that you were a slave in the land of Egypt, and the Lord your God redeemed you' (Deuteronomy 15.15).

5. There was a paste called *Charosheth*. It was made of apples, dates, pomegranates, and nuts, and through it there ran sticks of cinnamon. The paste was to remind them of the clay with which they had made bricks in Egypt, and the cinnamon was to remind them of the straw which was necessary to make the bricks, and which the Egyptians had withheld from them (Exodus 5.7–9).

6. Lastly, and very important, there were four cups of wine, each containing one-sixteenth of a *hin*, that is, a little more than half a pint of wine, diluted in the proportion of two parts of wine to three of water. They were so important that the poorest must have them, even if he had to be helped from the poor-box to buy them, and even if, as the Talmud says, a man had to pawn his coat, or hire himself out to get them. The four cups of wine were drunk at different points in the meal, and stood for the four promises of Exodus 6.6 f.:

I am the Lord, and I will bring you out from under the burdens of the Egyptians, and I will deliver you from their bondage, and I will redeem you with an outstretched arm and with great acts of judgment, and I will take you for my people, and I will be your God.

One thing is absolutely clear – from beginning to end the Passover meal was a commemoration of deliverance, of rescue and of redemption. We now turn to the meal itself.

1. It began with the first cup, the cup of the Kiddush, or the consecration. Certainly in later times, most likely even in the time of Jesus, the cup was accompanied with a prayer, thanking God for this memorial of redemption, and for taking Israel to himself as his own people.

2. There followed the first handwashing, in which only the person to preside ceremonially three times cleansed his hands.

3. Next a piece of lettuce or parsley was taken; it was then dipped into the salt water, and eaten. The lettuce or parsley stands for the hyssop which was dipped in the blood of the Passover lamb, and with which the lintel and the doorposts were smeared (Exodus 12.22), and the salt water stands, as we have seen, for either the tears of Egypt or the waters of the Red Sea.

4. Next there came the first breaking of bread. Three unleavened cakes of bread were in front of the host. The larger part was to be eaten later, but at this point he took the centre one, and broke it into little pieces.

The broken bread was to remind them of the bread of affliction which they ate in Egypt, and it was broken into little pieces to remind them that a slave never had a whole loaf, but only fragments to eat. In the full ritual of the Passover the host then says:

This is the bread of affliction which our forefathers ate in the land of Egypt. Whosoever is hungry, let him come and eat; whosoever is in need, let him come and eat the Passover with us.

It was, and is, at this point that the Jews of the Dispersion say: 'This year we eat it here, next year in Jerusalem.'

5. Next there came the proclaiming. It was the duty of the father to explain to his son what the Passover meal meant.

'And you shall tell your son on that day, It is because of what the Lord did for me when I came out of Egypt' (Exodus 13.8). In the full order for the Passover, here the youngest person present is to ask:

Why is this night different from other nights? For on all other nights we eat leavened or unleavened bread, but on this night only unleavened bread. On all other nights we eat any kind of herbs, but on this night only bitter herbs. On all other nights we eat meat roasted, stewed or boiled, but on this night only roasted.

In reply the father must begin at the saying in Deuteronomy 26.5: 'A wandering Aramaean was my father', and, beginning with Abraham, he must tell the story down to the deliverance of the Passover.

6. For the Jew, one of the most sacred parts of scripture, a part to be memorized in youth and never forgotten, is the Hallel. Hallel means 'Praise God', and the Hallel consists of Psalms 113–118, which are praising psalms. At this point the first two psalms of the Hallel, Psalms 113 and 114, are sung.

7. At this point the second cup is drunk. It is called the cup of the proclaiming, because it followed the proclaiming of the hand of God in Israel's history.

8. At this point all who were to participate cleansed their hands. This is the normal ceremonial handwashing before a meal, for now the meal proper was to begin.

9. First, grace was said, and small pieces of the unleavened bread were distributed to the company. The Passover grace is:

Blessed art thou, O Lord our God, who bringest forth fruit from the earth. Blessed art thou who hast sanctified us with thy commandment, and enjoined us to eat unleavened cakes.

10. Some more of the bitter herbs were then eaten, once again to waken the memory of their bitterness and of God's redemption from it.

11. There followed what was known as the sop. Some of the bitter herbs were placed between two pieces of Passover bread, dipped in the *charosheth* and eaten. Still again, memory is awakened.

It is here that the narrative of the Fourth Gospel takes a

Passover turn, for it is there said that Jesus dipped the morsel in the dish and gave it to Judas (John 13.26 f.). This looks like the taking and the giving of the sop.

12. Then the meal proper began. It was a meal of hungry men, for the rule was that no food might be eaten after the sacrifice of the lamb in the Temple, until the Passover meal itself, and the sacrifice could be as early as midday. As we have already noted, the whole lamb had to be eaten. Anything that remained had to be burned, for it could not be used for any ordinary purpose.

13. At the conclusion of the meal the hands were again ceremonially cleansed.

14. The remainder of the Passover bread was brought out and eaten.

15. There followed a long thanksgiving for the meal, which to this day contains a petition for the coming of Elijah as the herald of the Messiah.

16. After the thanksgiving prayer, the third cup, which was called the cup of thanksgiving, was drunk, with this prayer:

Blessed art thou, O Lord our God, King of the universe, who hast created the fruit of the vine.

17. The cup was filled for the fourth and last time. The second part of the Hallel, Psalms 115–118, was sung, and then the Great Hallel, Psalm 136, with its ever-recurring refrain: 'O give thanks to the Lord, for he is good, for his steadfast love endures for ever.' After that the fourth cup was drunk.

18. There follow two prayers. In the full ritual, the second of them runs as follows:

The breath of all that lives shall praise thy name, O Lord, our God. And the spirit of all flesh shall continually glorify and exalt thy memorial, O God, our King. For from everlasting to everlasting thou art God, and beside thee we have no king, redeemer, or saviour.

And so the Passover ends with a shout and a prayer of praise to God.

It can be seen at once that the keynotes of the Passover are memory, praise and hope, and it can also be seen that this well fits the occasion of the last meal of Jesus and his disciples. It can also be seen that the Synoptic narrative can fit into this scheme. Item 9 in our scheme could be the taking and blessing of the bread and the distributing of it. Then there would come the meal proper, item 12. The cup could be the cup of thanksgiving, item 16. And the concluding hymn (Mark 14.26; Matthew 26.30) could be the Great Hallel in whose praise the meal culminated. The sop can be referred to in the dipping of bread in the dish (Mark 14.20; Matthew 26.23). And the reference to the fruit of the vine (Mark 14.25; Matthew 26.29) comes very naturally from the thanksgiving for the third cup (item 16). The only thing in this reconstruction for which we need to go beyond the Synoptic Gospels is the information that the main meal did in fact intervene between the bread and the cup, as Paul tells us (I Corinthians 11.25).

Before we try to come to some decision between the Synoptics and John, let us look at certain views which hold that no such decision is necessary.

1. The most radical of all views is that the Last Supper has no historical foundation at all, and that therefore to discuss the date of it is to discuss something which does not in any event exist. This view holds that Christianity took over its common meal from the Greek Mystery cults, and then invented this story to give it a suitable origin. It is not possible to accept such scepticism, because the common meal is part of the fellowship of the Church as soon as the Church comes into view.

2. The second view is that there is no need to try either to harmonize the two Gospel traditions, or to decide between them, because both are right.[14] This has been argued on two grounds.

(*a*) Chwolson has argued that in the year of the death of Jesus the Passover fell on a Sabbath, which would involve serious complications with the Sabbath law. It is suggested that to avoid this the Pharisees and their supporters brought the Passover forward one day, so that it would fall on the

[14] Cf. the discussion in J. Jeremias, *The Eucharistic Words of Jesus* pp. 20–25.

Friday, and that it was that Passover which Jesus and his disciples observed. On the other hand, it is suggested that the Sadducees, who were the priestly party, left the Passover on the Sabbath, and that it was that Passover which those who would not enter Pilate's judgment seat were going to observe. This suggests that in the year of Jesus' death, since the Passover feel on a Sabbath, there were actually two celebrations of it, one by the Pharisaic party and one by the Sadducean party; and that it is the Pharisaic celebration which is described in the Synoptic Gospels, while it is the Sadducean celebration which in the Fourth Gospel is still to come.

(*b*) Strack and Billerbeck have argued that in the year of Jesus' crucifixion there was unsettled debate between the Pharisees and the Sadducees as to the date when the month of Nisan actually began. The Pharisees began the month one day earlier than the Sadducees did. This of course complicated the date of the Passover, and it is argued that for this one year the Passover was held on two consecutive days, preceded on each day by the sacrifice of the lambs. It is then suggested, as in the previous theory, that the Synoptics tell of a celebration by Jesus and his disciples on the earlier Pharisaic date, and that the Fourth Gospel refers to the Sadducean date which was still to come.

There is no doubt that these are ingenious theories, and there is little doubt that what they suggest could have happened. But in fact they are pure speculation, and there is no evidence at all that it did. To accept either of these theories we would need better evidence than can be produced.

So we cannot accept the view that the account of the Lord's Supper is a completely unhistorical production of the Church, constructed to provide authority for a rite that was already in use, and which had come from Hellenistic Mystery religion practice. Nor can we accept the view that the divergence between the Synoptic Gospels and the Fourth Gospel is due to the fact that in that year the Passover Festival was kept on two successive days. We are thus compelled to come to a decision between the two accounts. Let us, then, see what factors in the situation can be taken to argue for the last meal being a

Passover meal, and what factors can be used to argue that it was not.[15]

First, we shall take the indications that the meal was a Passover meal.

1. Although Jesus was staying in Bethany,[16] the meal was eaten in Jerusalem, and it was in Jerusalem that the Passover must be eaten,[17] for it was one of the three festivals – the other two were Pentecost and Tabernacles – which were obligatory.[18]

2. It was eaten late in the evening.[19] The Passover meal had to be eaten between 6 p.m. and midnight. This was much later than an ordinary meal, which would have been eaten in the later part of the afternoon.

3. It was eaten reclining.[20] The original Passover was eaten standing, ready for the road,[21] but once the people were settled in the Promised Land it was the rule that the Passover should be eaten reclining, to show that they had 'passed from slavery to freedom'.[22]

4. The meal in the Upper Room did not begin with the breaking of bread as an ordinary meal would have begun. The breaking of bread took place in the course of the meal.[23] This suits the Passover ritual.

5. Wine was drunk at the meal.[24] At the Passover this was obligatory; it would have been less likely at an ordinary meal.

6. The poor were remembered.[25] This was standard practice at the Passover time, when the poor were helped to buy the wine and when those who had nothing were invited to share the feast.[26] It would not have been so natural to make such provision at an ordinary meal. This is in fact one of the hints that even the narrative of the Fourth Gospel has behind it a tradition involving the Passover.

7. The meal ended with the singing of a hymn,[27] and the

---

[15] For a full treatment see J. Jeremias, *The Eucharistic Words of Jesus*, pp. 41–84, and for a good summary see Vincent Taylor, *The Gospel according to St. Mark*, pp. 664–667.

[16] Mark 11.11.   [17] Deuteronomy 16.5.   [18] Exodus 23.14–17.

[19] Mark 14.17; Matthew 26.20; I Corinthians 11.23.

[20] Mark 14.18, *anakeimenōn autōn*.   [21] Exodus 12.11.

[22] R. Levi in j. Pesahim 10.37b.   [23] Mark 14.22; Matthew 26.26.

[24] Mark 14.23; Matthew 26.27.   [25] John 13.29.   [26] Pesahim 10.1.

[27] Mark 14.26; Matthew 26.30.

Passover meal ended with the singing of part of the Hallel, and of the Great Hallel.[28]

8. The Last Supper included explanations of certain things that Jesus did, and the Passover meal too included instruction in its meaning.[29]

It can be seen that the Last Supper corresponds in many details with the Passover ritual.

Let us now turn to the factors in the story which are used as arguments that the Last Supper was not a Passover meal.

1. It has been stated that the bread which Jesus took into his hands at the Last Supper is *artos*, which, it is claimed, must mean ordinary bread, and not *azuma*, which is unleavened bread. But the fact is that *artos* in Greek, like *lehem* in Hebrew, can mean both kinds of bread. For instance, in the Septuagint and in the New Testament the Bread of the Presence, or the Shewbread, is called *artos*, and it was unleavened.[30] The Nazirite offering was of unleavened cakes and wafers, and yet the Septuagint calls it *artos*.[31] Philo actually calls the Passover bread itself *artos*.[32] From the fact that the bread of the Last Supper is called *artos*, nothing against a Passover celebration can be deduced.

2. In the narrative of the Last Supper there is no mention of the lamb. This at first sight is strange, but the obvious explanation is that only those parts of the Passover ritual which Jesus took over and used for his own purposes are recorded.

3. Two objections may be taken together. It is claimed that at the Passover time Simon of Cyrene could not have been coming into the city from the country,[33] for such a journey would have been forbidden; and it is also claimed that Jesus and his disciples could not have gone out to the Garden of Gethsemane, for the regulation was that no one should leave the city until after the feast was ended. But such were the numbers of pilgrims who came to the Passover that lodging for them was not nearly sufficient. So the area of the city was technically expanded to include what might be called Great Jerusalem,

[28] Pesahim 10.7.   [29] Pesahim 9.4.
[30] Exodus 25.30; Mark 2.26; Matthew 12.4; Luke 6.4.
[31] Numbers 6.15.   [32] Philo, *De Spec. Leg.* 2.158.   [33] Mark 15.21.

reaching right out to Bethphage.[34] Within that area a man might move, and outside it he might reside during the festival, so long as he ate the Passover meal within the city proper. With regard to Simon, Jeremias well points out that in any case Simon may not have been a Jew at all, and that Jewish regulations may well have had nothing to do with him anyway.[35]

4. It is claimed that during the Passover time arms could not be carried, and it is pointed out that the Temple police came armed to arrest Jesus.[36] It is certainly the general case that arms could not be carried, but the Mishnah proves that this regulation was not in fact universally accepted.[37]

5. It is claimed that the trial of Jesus could not possibly have been held within the Passover season, because during that season it would have been illegal to carry it out. But there is one exception to that. Even during the great Festivals a false prophet could be tried, so that all the people should hear and fear. Further, the passage from Deuteronomy was quoted: 'The hand of the witnesses shall be first against him to put him to death, and afterward the hand of all the people', and it was pointed out that only at the great festivals were all the people in fact present.[38] Since Jesus was regarded as a false prophet, his trial during the Passover time was not illegal.

6. It is claimed that the preparations for burial, for instance Joseph's purchase of a linen shroud and the preparation of the spices and the ointments, would not have been legal within the Passover season when all trading was forbidden.[39] But it is expressly laid down in the Mishnah that all that is needful for burial may be done on the Sabbath.[40]

7. C. H. Turner points out that in the Eastern Church the Eucharist has always been celebrated with unleavened bread, and suggests that this implies that it was not originally a Passover meal.[41] But this may well have been simply a matter of convenience.

It would seem on balance that the evidence that the Last

[34] See J. Jeremias, *The Eucharistic Words of Jesus*, p. 43, note 2.
[35] J. Jeremias, *op. cit.*, p. 77.   [36] Mark 14.43; Matthew 26.47.
[37] *Shabbath* 6.4.   [38] *Sanhedrin* 11.4; Deuteronomy 17.7, 13.
[39] Mark 15.46; Luke 23.56.   [40] *Shabbath* 23.4, 5.
[41] C. H. Turner, *St Mark*, p. 67.

Supper was a Passover meal is stronger than the evidence that it was not, and that the objections which are raised to its Passover character can be met.

Before we try to come to a decision as to whether or not the Last Supper was a Passover meal, there is one other question that it would be well to ask. If it was not a Passover meal, what could it have been?[42] There are three main possibilities.

1. It is suggested that it may have been a Kiddush. A *kiddush* means a consecrating, a sanctifying, a hallowing. The commandment gave its instruction to remember the Sabbath day, to keep it holy (Exodus 20.8). The basic meaning of 'holy' is 'different', 'separate', 'set apart.' And the Kiddush was a ceremony by which the Sabbath was set apart. The outline of the Kiddush is as follows.

The first Sabbath ceremony is the lighting of the Sabbath light. As the woman of the house lights the Sabbath lamp, she prays: 'Blessed art thou, O Lord, our King, King of the universe, who hast sanctified us by thy commandments, and commanded us to light the Sabbath lamp.'

Then there comes the Kiddush meal. On the table there is a white cloth and in front of the father's place there are two loaves of bread, specially baked, and standing for the double portion of manna which had to be gathered before the Sabbath day began.[43] Beside them there is a jug of wine and an empty cup.

First, the father reads from Genesis the story of the sixth and seventh day of creation. Then he fills the cup, and, as he holds it, he prays:

Blessed art thou, O Lord our God, King of the universe, the creator of the fruit of the vine. Blessed art thou, O Lord our God, King of the universe, who hast sanctified us by thy commandments, and wast pleased with us, and hast given us for a heritage in love and favour, thy holy Sabbath, a memorial of the work of creation. For it precedes all the holy convocations, in memory of the going forth from Egypt. For thou hast chosen us, and hast hallowed us above all nations, and hast given us in love and favour thy holy

---

[42] The alternatives are fully discussed in J. Jeremias, *The Eucharistic Words of Jesus*, pp. 26–36.
[43] Exodus 16.22.

Sabbath for a heritage. Blessed art thou, O Lord, who hallowest the Sabbath.

The father then drinks from the cup, and passes it round the family, and even the women and the children partake of it. Then the hands are washed. The Psalmist said: 'I wash my hands in innocence.'[44]

Then the bread is blessed:

Blessed art thou, O Lord our God, King of the universe, who bringest forth bread from the earth.

Then the bread is broken and shared out. This is the full ceremony, as it is carried out today; it was much simpler in the time of Jesus.

Two things have been supposed. First, it has been supposed that there was a Kiddush for the Passover time. Second, it has been supposed that what Jesus and his disciples did was to hold, not the Passover, but the Kiddush, while the Passover itself was not due until the next night. Jeremias holds that this involves two impossibilities. First, the Kiddush was always associated with the Sabbath. 'A separation of the Kiddush . . . from the sacred day is absolutely unthinkable and without example.'[45] Second, a Kiddush was never held, so to speak, in advance. It was held immediately before the Sabbath began. Even if there was by any chance a Passover Kiddush, it would be immediately before the Feast, not on the evening of the day before.

2. It is suggested that the Last Supper was what was called a *chaburah* meal. A *chaburah* was a society of like-minded people. The Pharisees, for instance, called themselves a *chaburah*. Such societies sometimes had meals together. It is suggested that Jesus and the Twelve constituted a *chaburah*, and that this was their fellowship meal. But Jeremias points out[46] that these *chaburah* meals were always 'duty' meals, and were always connected with circumcision, or betrothal, or a wedding or a funeral, and that the guests at them were paying-

---

[44] Psalm 26.6.   [45] J. Jeremias, *The Eucharistic Words of Jesus*, p. 26.
[46] Ibid., pp. 30 f.

guests. The *chaburah* meal does not really meet the circumstances of the Last Supper at all.

We have now come to a point at which we have no alternative to deciding between the account of the Synoptic Gospels and the account of the Fourth Gospel. We may best come at an answer to this by asking two interrelated questions. First, if the Synoptic account is historically correct, how did the account of the Fourth Gospel arise? Second, if the account of the Fourth Gospel is historically correct, how did the account in the Synoptics arise?

1. First, then, if the account in the Synoptic Gospels is historically accurate, how are we to account for the version of the Fourth Gospel? It has been said that the Fourth Gospel is more interested in truth than in facts – and there is as much truth in this saying as there is in most epigrams. Now the Fourth Gospel does see Jesus as the lamb of God. 'Behold, the lamb of God, who takes away the sin of the world!'[47] It can be argued that John's passion narrative is designed exactly to show Jesus in this character. According to Mark the crucifixion was carried out at nine o'clock in the morning.[48] According to John the decision to crucify Jesus was taken by Pilate at twelve o'clock midday.[49] Now in John's narrative the Passover is still to come; it is still the Preparation for the Passover, and at twelve o'clock midday on the day of Preparation the slaughter and sacrifice of the lambs had just begun in the Temple. As John has it, Jesus was handed over to be crucified at the exact time when the Passover lambs were beginning to be sacrificed in the Temple. Once again, Jesus is shown as the lamb of God.

But we have another discrepancy between the accounts of the Synoptic Gospels and the Fourth Gospel. In the Synoptic Gospels the anointing at Bethany takes place two days before the Passover.[50] In these Gospels, the anointing is a symbolic preparation of the body of Jesus for its burial.[51] In the Fourth Gospel the anointing takes place six days before the Passover.[52]

[47] John 1.29, 36.   [48] Mark 15.25.   [49] John 19.14.
[50] Mark 14.1; Matthew 26.2.   [51] Mark 14.8; Matthew 26.12.
[52] John 12.1.

Now it was the original custom that the lamb for the Passover was chosen six days ahead, and for these six days was kept tethered at the door of the house. It may well be that John is seeing the anointing at Bethany as the symbolic choosing of Jesus as the Passover lamb. Once again, Jesus is being shown as the lamb of God.

In still another incident this motif recurs. In order to hasten the death of the crucified victims their legs were broken. In the case of Jesus this was not necessary because he was already dead. And this is taken as a fulfilment of the saying: 'Not a bone of him shall be broken'.[53] Now in point of fact 'not a bone of him shall be broken' is part of the prescription for the treatment and preparation of the Passover lamb.[54] Once again, Jesus is shown as the Passover lamb. In the case of the Fourth Gospel it is easy to see how the rearrangement of the timing could have taken place in order to show Jesus as the Passover lamb, the lamb of God who takes away the sin of the world. And this would be fully in line with Paul's saying: 'Christ, our paschal lamb, has been sacrificed.'[55]

2. We now ask how the Synoptic account could have arisen, if the narrative of the Fourth Gospel is historically correct. This is much harder to explain. The best explanation is that given by C. H. Turner.[56] It is a lengthy passage, but it has to be quoted in full:

Let us cast our thoughts back to the first Good Friday evening. Can we suppose that Peter and his fellow-disciples, at the moment when their Master had just been put to a shameful death, proceeded to celebrate the Paschal meal? Must they not rather, instead of keeping the feast, have fasted and wept, and dwelt rather on the meal of the preceding evening when he had last eaten with them and had left them the Memorial of the New Covenant in his blood? What it all meant they did not yet realize: but either all the faith and hope they had cherished had crumbled to dust, or something had happened which was radically to transform the Old Covenant and its rites. Pass on a year: as Nisan 14–15 came round again, were the disciples to think of the Jewish Passover, or of the death of Jesus and of its meaning for them and for Israel and for the world?

[53] John 19.31–36.
[54] Exodus 12.46; Numbers 9.12.
[55] I Corinthians 5.7.
[56] C. H. Turner, *St Mark*, p. 67.

C

Were they to feast or fast 'in that day when the bridegroom' had been 'taken from them'? Is it overbold to suggest that they may have treated the preceding evening, that of the Last Supper, as the Jewish Pascha, and then on Nisan 14–15 have kept the Christian Pascha, the fast that ended in the Easter feast? If this were so, we can easily see how easily the phraseology would grow up which spoke of the Last Supper as a Passover.

To put it briefly, Turner suggests that in the year Jesus died the disciples in their despair never kept the Passover at all. But when in the next year the Passover came round again, their one memory of the last Passover was in fact the last meal in the Upper Room. For them it had been the Passover, and in their minds it was for ever and inextricably bound up with the Passover. They looked back on it as their Passover, and so came to identify the Passover and the last meal.

It is an ingenious and a beautiful theory. In the last analysis any judgment on this problem must be subjective, one man's judgment. And to ourselves it is much easier to think of John writing his narrative to show Jesus as the lamb of God than to think of the disciples making this kind of transference of date. The rearrangement is so characteristic of John that we believe he rearranged his material to show Jesus as the lamb slain for the sins of the world. And we believe that factual history is with the Synoptic narrative, and that the Last Supper was a Passover meal.

3

THE PROBLEM OF WORDS

IT is an extraordinary fact that, although the Sacrament of the Lord's Supper is the central act of the Church's worship, the identification of the words of its institution presents a tangled, and perhaps even an insoluble, problem. This problem would remain for even the most determined fundamentalist, who insisted on taking the words of scripture exactly as they stand, for he, as much as anyone else, would have to decide which version of the words as they stand he proposed to take. Since this is so we begin by setting down the different versions of the words of the institution in a translation as nearly literal as possible. The words are in Mark 14.22–25; Matthew 26.26–29; Luke 22.15–20; I Corinthians 11.23–25.

Mark 14.22–25	*Matthew 26.26–29*
22 While they were eating, having taken bread, having blessed it, he broke it, and gave it to them, and said: Take, this is my body.	26 While they were eating, Jesus, having taken bread, and having blessed it, broke it, and, having given it to the disciples, said: Take, eat, this is my body.
23 And having taken a cup, having given thanks, he gave it to them, and they all drank from it.	27 And, having taken a (the) cup, and having given thanks, he gave it to them, saying: All of you drink from it.
24 And he said to them: This is my blood of the (new) covenant, which is being poured out for many.	28 For this is my blood of the (new) covenant, which is being poured out for many, for the remission of sins.

25 Truly, I tell you, I shall not drink (again) of the fruit of the vine, until that day, when I drink it new in the kingdom of God.

29 I tell you, from now on, I shall not drink of this fruit of the vine, until that day, when I drink it with you new in the kingdom of my Father.

Luke 22.15–20   Five texts

The Longer Text

15 I have greatly desired to eat this Passover meal with you, before I suffer.

16 For I tell you I will not eat it (again) until it is fulfilled in the kingdom of God.

17 And having received a cup, having given thanks, he said:
Take this, and divide it among yourselves.

18 For I tell you that from this present time, I will not drink from the fruit of the vine, until the kingdom of God comes.

19 And having taken bread, having given thanks, he broke it and gave it to them, saying:
This is my body, which is given for you.
Do this to the remembering of me.

20 In the same way, the cup after the meal was finished, saying:
This cup *is* the new covenant in my blood, which is being poured out for you.

Short Text

In D and some Latin MSS

17 And having received a cup, having given thanks, he said:
Take this and divide it among yourselves.

18 For I tell you that from this present time, I will not drink from the fruit of the vine, until the Kingdom of God comes.

19a And having taken bread, having given thanks, he broke *it*, and gave *it* to them saying:
This is my body.

Short Text

In the Curetonian Syriac

19a And having taken bread, having given thanks, he broke it, and gave it to them, saying:
This is my body.

17 And having received a cup, having given thanks, he said:
Take this and divide it among yourselves.

18 For I tell you that from this present time, I will not drink from the fruit of the vine, until the kingdom of God comes.

Short Text

Philoxenian Syriac and some Coptic MSS

19 And having taken bread, having given thanks, he broke *it* and gave *it* to them, saying:
This is my body,
which is given for you.
Do this to the remembering of me.

20 In the same way the cup after the meal was finished, saying:
This cup is the new covenant in my blood,
which is being poured out for you.

Short Text

Sinaitic Syriac

19 And having taken bread, having given thanks, he broke it and gave it to them, saying:
This is my body,
which is given for you.
Do this to the remembering of me.

20a In the same way, the cup after the meal was finished.

17 And having received a cup, having given thanks, he said:
Take this and divide it among yourselves.

20b This my blood *is* the new covenant, which is being poured out for you.

18 For I tell you that from this present time, I will not drink from the fruit of the vine, until the kingdom of God comes.

I Corinthians 11.23–25

23 The Lord Jesus on the night he was being betrayed took bread,

24 And having given thanks, he broke it and said:
This is my body which is for you.
(Some MSS read: which is broken (*klōmenon* or *thruptomenon*) for you.
Others read: which is being given for you.

Others read: which I have delivered (*tradidi*) for you.)
Do this to the remembering of me.

25 In the same way, the cup too after the meal was finished, saying:
This cup is the new covenant in my blood.
Do this as often as you drink it to the remembering of me.

It can be seen that Luke presents a special problem. In Luke there is a long and a short text. The AV gives the long text:

15 And he said unto them, With desire I have desired to eat this
16 passover with you before I suffer: For I say unto you, I will not any more eat thereof, until it be fulfilled in the kingdom of God.
17 And he took the cup, and gave thanks, and said, Take this and
18 divide *it* among yourselves: For I say unto you, I will not drink of the fruit of the vine, until the kingdom of God shall come.
19 And he took bread, and gave thanks, and brake *it*, and gave unto them, saying, This is my body which is given for you: this
20 do in remembrance of me. Likewise also the cup after supper, saying, This cup *is* the new testament in my blood, which is shed for you.

The RSV gives the short text, as does the NEB:

15 And he said to them, 'I have earnestly desired to eat this pass-
16 over with you before I suffer; for I tell you I shall not eat it
17 until it is fulfilled in the kingdom of God.' And he took a cup, and when he had given thanks he said, 'Take this, and divide it
18 among yourselves; for I tell you that from now on I shall not drink of the fruit of the vine until the kingdom of God comes.'
19 And he took bread, and when he had given thanks he broke it and gave it to them, saying, 'This is my body'.

The short text omits the second half of verse 19 and the whole of verse 20. But this is not all. The versions, notably the Syriac versions, of Luke have no fewer than three different rearrangements of the text. The Curetonian Syriac has the verses in the order 19a, 17, 18, with 19b and 20 omitted. The Philoxenian Syriac, with some Coptic manuscripts, has only verses 19 and 20. The Sinaitic Syriac has the verses in the order 19, 20a, 17, 20b, 18. What these versions are trying to do is clear enough. They are trying to avoid a sequence in which there are two cups, or in which the cup comes before the bread.

Now clearly, when we have to decide between two different readings, our decision will depend on the value we attach to the manuscripts in which the different readings are. Well, then, what is the manuscript evidence for the long and the short readings? In the United Bible Societies' new text of the Greek

New Testament there are quoted in favour of the *longer* text one papyrus manuscript, fourteen uncial manuscripts, two families of manuscripts, nineteen minuscule manuscripts, the majority consensus opinion of both the Byzantine manuscripts and the lectionaries, five old Latin manuscripts, the Vulgate, one version of the Syriac version, the Egyptian versions, and the Armenian and the Georgian versions. In other words, there are few better attested readings in the New Testament than the longer text. For the shorter text there are quoted one single uncial manuscript, five Old Latin manuscripts, and one version of the Syriac version. In other words, numerically the witnesses for the shorter text are almost negligible.

Why then do the newer translations of the New Testament, the RSV and the NEB, choose the shorter text in spite of this manuscript evidence? They do so for three reasons. First, there is a principle of textual criticism which says that the shorter reading is always likely to be right. This is so because a scribe was much more likely to add new material than to omit existing material. A scribe would seldom take something out, but he would often put something in. Therefore, generally speaking, a short text is more likely to be original than a long text, because the long text is likely to be the short one with extra material added to it later. Second, there is a principle that the more difficult reading is always likely to be right. A scribe would not alter an easy reading, but he might well try to make a difficult reading more easy to understand. In this case the short text is certainly more difficult, because it puts the cup before the bread, which is quite unusual. Third, the one manuscript in which the short reading occurs is an odd manuscript. Its name is Codex Bezae and its symbol is D. Now one of the characteristics of this manuscript is that it adds new material. For instance, in Acts, it adds so much new material that some people think that it is no less than another edition of Acts. Any omission in a manuscript given to addition is doubly significant. A scribe who was an inveterate and characteristic and constitutional adder would hardly be likely to be a subtracter. Therefore, so it is claimed, the shorter text must be right.

Jeremias does not agree that these arguments are final, nor does he accept the short text as original.[1] Nor do we. We do not believe even on the strength of the arguments stated that it is reasonable to reject the evidence of all other manuscripts for the evidence of one. This is asking too much. It is in effect asking that what looks very like a freak reading should be chosen as the only right reading. We do not believe that the weight of the manuscript evidence can be rejected.

But we must then explain how the shorter text arose. There are two possibilities. The scribe of D did not copy his manuscript from one continuous manuscript of the New Testament. He most likely used different manuscripts for different parts of the New Testament; and his manuscript for Luke–Acts was not the same as his manuscript or manuscripts for the other Gospels. In his Luke original there are two possible happenings. First, it was common practice in liturgical manuscripts to quote only the beginning of a paragraph to save space, especially when the rest of the paragraph was well known. So the opening words were quoted with the letters *ktl*, which are the Greek for *etc*. The scribe of D may have been copying from such a manuscript here, a manuscript which gave an abbreviated version of the words of institution, because they were so well known. Second, it is possible that the manuscript from which the scribe copied was originally a manuscript which did not give the full words of the institution, because they were regarded as the *arcana*, the secret words, of the Christian sacrament, which was only for believers. He did not want them to fall into the hands of, and quite likely to be misinterpreted by, heathen.

Whatever the reason for the shorter text, it cannot displace the longer text, which has such almost unanimous manuscript support, and in our consideration of the words of the institution of the Lord's Supper we propose to use the longer text of Luke as the original text.

Let us then see if we can come to any conclusion about what the original form of the words of the institution was. We can for the moment leave aside the words of Jesus which were in

[1] J. Jeremias, *The Eucharistic Words of Jesus*, pp. 139–160.

the nature of instruction to the disciples, words like, 'Take, eat,'[2] as being comparatively unimportant, and we can concentrate on the words which he spoke about his own actions.

The word about the bread

First, we take the word about the bread.[3] In our four sources that word is as follows:

Mark: This is my body.
Matthew: This is my body.
Luke: This is my body which is given for you.
I Corinthians: This is my body which is for you.

In the Corinthians passage this is the reading of the oldest and best manuscripts. A number of manuscripts have *broken for you* (*klōmenon*). Some of these manuscripts originally had simply *for you*, and later correctors inserted the word *broken*. One manuscript has *thruptomenon*, which means rather *crushed*, instead of *broken*. Some versions have *given*, as in Luke. And some Old Latin manuscripts have, *which I have delivered* (*tradidi*) *for you*.

When we look at these various forms and readings, a fairly certain conclusion emerges. We can see here three stages of development. *1.* There is the simple saying: This is my body. *2.* To it there is added in Paul the additional and explanatory phrase: Which is for you. That this phrase is a later addition is highly likely. Jesus spoke Aramaic, and the words of the institution at the first Lord's Supper were in Aramaic; and it is the opinion of the Aramaic experts that this phrase, 'which is for you', will not translate back into Aramaic.[4] This phrase, then, is an interpretation, and a correct interpretation, of the short and simple statement of Jesus. *3.* The third stage is the stage at which the phrase *which is for you* is still further amplified by the addition of the word *broken* or *given*, again a correct interpretation, and added for the sake of clarity. We may be

[2] Mark 14.22; Matthew 26.26.
[3] Mark 14.22; Matthew 26.26; Luke 22.19; I Corinthians 11.24.
[4] A. J. B. Higgins, *The Lord's Supper in the New Testament*, p. 29; J. Jeremias, *The Eucharistic Words of Jesus*, p. 167; G. Dalman, *Jesus-Jeshua*, ET, pp. 144 f.

fairly confident that the word about the bread in the original institution was simply: This is my body.

The word about the cup

The word about the cup does not present so easy a solution since in our sources there is greater variation.[5]

Mark: This is my blood of the covenant, which is poured out for many.

Matthew: This is my blood of the covenant, which is poured out for many for the forgiveness of sins.

Luke: This cup which is poured out for you is the new covenant in my blood.

I Corinthians: This cup is the new covenant in my blood.

In both Matthew and Mark, the later manuscripts usually add *new* to the word covenant, thus bringing the phrase into line with Luke and Paul.

The original form of this saying is much in dispute. It is pointed out that in Mark and in Matthew *my blood of the covenant* is an awkward phrase in any language. And it is also pointed out that the neatest form of the phrase is that found in I Corinthians. This has led some scholars to point out that the covenant idea is the basis of the thought of Paul.[6]

It has therefore been suggested that here two forms of this saying have come together. *1.* There is the form which lies at the back of Mark and Matthew, and which began with the simple saying, exactly parallel to the saying about the bread, *This is my blood*, to which the explanatory phrases *which is poured out for many* and *for the forgiveness of sins* were later added as perfectly correct and helpful interpretations. *2.* There is the form which lies at the back of Paul, or which is actually in Paul, in which the covenant idea becomes the dominant idea, and in which the death of Jesus is looked on as the inauguration of the new covenant, and in particular the fulfilment of

[5] Mark 14.24; Matthew 26. 28; Luke 22.20; I Corinthians 11.25.
[6] Cf. Romans 9.4; 11.27; II Corinthians 3.6; Galatians 3.17; 4.24; Ephesians 2.12. A. J. B. Higgins, *The Lord's Supper in the New Testament*, p. 34.

Jeremiah 31.31–34. *3*. There then comes the third stage when the covenant theme is combined with the form in Matthew and Mark, and to the originally simple *This is my blood* there is added *of the covenant*. This, it is suggested, is the history of the formation of this saying.

That would mean that the covenant idea is not part of the original words of Jesus at all. A. J. B. Higgins writes: 'We have, then, no evidence that at his last meal with his disciples Jesus spoke of a new covenant, or, indeed, that he spoke of a covenant at all.'[7] Before we can accept this view of the matter, it is necessary that we should look more closely at the cup words. Let us set it down in Mark's form:

This is my blood of the covenant which is poured out for many.

1. We begin by noting that the origin of the phrase is undoubtedly Isaiah's description of the Servant:

He poured out his soul to death.[8]

At the back of this there is the picture of the Suffering Servant, whose sufferings and death were for the sake of others.

2. *Which is poured out*. In Greek this is the present participle, *ekchunnomenon*.[9] At first sight we would at once translate this: *which is being poured out for many*, but Jeremias[10] correctly points out that, unlike Greek, Hebrew and Aramaic have no participial forms which distinguish time. 'The participle is atemporal. Its time sphere is determined by the context.' The participle can therefore regularly be used of an event soon to come in the near future. This will therefore rather mean *which is soon to be shed for you*. This is not in fact un-Greek. There is in Greek what might be called the imminent present. In the RSV, Revelation 2.5 reads: 'I will come to you.' In the Greek the verb is in the present tense (*erchomai*), 'I am coming.' Here there is the same imminent use of the present participle.

3. *For many*. It would be easy to extract a wrong meaning, and a whole wrong theology, from these words. Jeremias dis-

[7] A. J. B. Higgins, *The Lord's Supper in the New Testament*, p. 34.
[8] Isaiah 53.12.
[9] Mark 14.24; Matthew 26.28; Luke 22.20.
[10] J. Jeremias, *The Eucharistic Words of Jesus*, p. 178.

cusses their meaning at length.[11] The point at issue is that in English *many* is *exclusive*, and differentiated from *all*; in Hebrew it is *inclusive*, and is equivalent to *all*. This is partly because the Hebrew word for *all* (*kol*, Aramaic: *kolla*) has no plural, because it describes a thing in its totality, but not as the sum of its different parts. It is *whole* rather than *all*. Even in English, *the many*, the *hoi polloi*, which is in any event the Greek for the many, means the mob, the mass, of the ordinary people. So in Hebrew *hārabbīm*, literally *the many*, regularly means the whole community. In the Mishnah tractate *Aboth*, the *Sayings of the Fathers*, we read:

Moses was virtuous and led the many to virtue; the virtue of the many depended on him, as it is written, He executed the justice of the Lord and his judgments with Israel. Jeroboam sinned and he led the many to sin; the sin of the many depended on him, as it is written, For the sins of Jeroboam which he sinned and wherewith he made Israel to sin.[12]

There is no doubt that there *the many* equals Israel, the nation, the whole community, all.

This usage comes into the New Testament. In Romans, Paul writes: 'As by one man's disobedience many were made sinners, so by one man's obedience many will be made righteous.'[13] Clearly, through Adam's sin, *all* were made sinners. This is in fact what Paul says in I Corinthians: 'For as in Adam all die, so also in Christ shall all be made alive.'[14]

Even when the definite article is omitted and it is simply *many* instead of *the many*, the sense is still often *all*. Isaiah has: 'He bore the sin of many',[15] and John, remembering the phrase, has it that the lamb of God takes away the sin of the world.[16] Mark says that the Son of Man came to give his life a ransom for many,[17] while I Timothy says that he gave himself a ransom for *all*.[18] And both mean the same, for Mark's *many* is a Hebraism for the Greek *all* in I Timothy.

So then, when the blood of Jesus is said to be poured out for

[11] *Op. cit.*, pp. 179–182.
[12] *Aboth* 5.18; H. Danby, *The Mishnah*, p. 458.
[13] Romans 5.19.   [14] I Corinthians 15.22.   [15] Isaiah 53.12.
[16] John 1.29.   [17] Mark 10.45.   [18] I Timothy 2.6.

many, this is not selective and exclusive; it is inclusive, and the meaning is *for all*.

4. *My blood of the covenant*. Greek not uncommonly uses the genitive of a noun instead of an adjective. So 'sons of disobedience' are disobedient sons.[19] 'The body of this death' is this deadly body.[20] So, then, 'the blood of the covenant' is covenant blood. The covenant needs the blood to ratify it.[21] The covenant is, as it were, signed and sealed in blood. And the new covenant is made possible because of the blood, the life and death, of Jesus.

5. But we have to look at the Pauline version of the cup saying:

This cup is the new covenant in my blood.[22]

There are two questions here which we must ask concerning meaning. What is the meaning of the word *covenant*? A covenant is a relationship of friendship into which two people enter, with mutual pledges of fidelity. In the New Testament the covenant is the relationship between God and his people, and the basis of that relationship was, first, the approach of God to Israel, and, second, the agreement of Israel to keep the law.[23] Moses read the law and the people agreed to keep it. This is of the very essence of Jewish religion.

To break the law was to break the covenant relationship. Man, being man, did break the law, and it was to restore the lost relationship that the whole system of sacrifice was developed. The covenant is a relationship between God and his people, the people Israel. It is dependent on the keeping of the law. The law is inevitably broken, and the relationship interrupted. The sacrificial system is the means whereby the breach is atoned for and the relationship restored, always with the proviso that the sacrifice was futile without the penitence of the man on whose behalf it was offered.

The second question is, What is the meaning of the phrase *in my blood*? The Hebrew word *b* (the *e* is pronounced as in *the*) means *at the price of*, and it is frequently translated by the

[19] Ephesians 2.2; 5.6; Colossians 3.6.   [20] Romans 7.24.
[21] Exodus 24.1–8.   [22] I Corinthians 11.25.   [23] Exodus 24.7.

Greek word *en*, the word which is used here in the phrase usually translated *in* my blood; and it is true that the basic meaning of *en* is *in*. David demands Michal to wife, for he has betrothed her at the price of a hundred foreskins of the Philistines.[24] *At the price of* is in Hebrew *bᵉ*, and in the Greek of the Septuagint *en*. David will not accept the threshing-floor of Araunah for nothing. He will buy it *for* a price.[25] *For* is in Hebrew *bᵉ* and in Greek *en*. I would suggest that the *en* in the phrase *in my blood* means *at the price of my blood*, and that the whole phrase means: 'This cup stands for the relationship with God made possible at the price of my blood.' The covenant blood is the blood which makes the covenant possible, the price of the relationship.

Now that we have more closely established the meaning of the words concerning the cup, we are in a better position to decide in what form they go back to Jesus.

One thing stands out – the word about the cup would require much more explanation than the word about the bread, because of the peculiar Jewish attitude to blood. That attitude is made clear in the Law:

> If any man of the house of Israel or of the strangers that sojourn among them eats any blood, I will set my face against that person who eats blood, and will cut him off from among his people. For the life of the flesh is in the blood: and I have given it for you upon the altar to make atonement for your souls; for it is the blood that makes atonement, by reason of the life. Therefore I have said to the people of Israel, No person among you shall eat blood, neither shall any stranger who sojourns among you eat blood.[26]

For this very reason the cup saying has always been difficult for Jews. C. G. Montefiore in his commentary on Mark wrote of the difficulty in believing it possible 'that a Palestinian or Galilaean Jew could have suggested that in drinking wine his disciples were, even symbolically, drinking blood. For the horror with which the drinking of blood was regarded by the Jews is well known.' H. Loewe writes: 'Jews shudder at certain passages in Hebrews and Romans, and the Gospel verses

[24] II Samuel 3.14.   [25] II Samuel 24.24.   [26] Leviticus 17.10–12.

describing the institution of the Eucharist are painfully repugnant to them.'[27] In view of this it is in the last degree improbable that Jesus said barely: 'This is my blood.' There must have been explanation.

Now let us see what the additions are. The blood, said Jesus, is *poured out for all*. This, as we have seen, goes back to Isaiah 53.12, and begins by putting the matter into that sphere of thought in which the idea of the Suffering Servant moves. This would be entirely in line with the thought of Jesus. Now, unless we deny altogether that Jesus had any idea what he was doing, he must have regarded his death as more than a mere human disaster. He lived, and he ultimately died, to bring men into a new relationship with God, that relationship whose key word is Father. To any Jew, that relationship would be thought of in covenant terms. There is therefore every reason to believe that Jesus did think of his death as a sacrificial act inaugurating a new covenant, and since it was not legally based, it was for all. So when Jesus bade his disciples drink of that cup, he was not asking them to drink his blood; he was asking them always to remember how his sacrificial death was the culmination of a life, which did in fact change the relationship between man and God.

If Jesus knew what he was doing, if he was conscious of any object in his life and death at all, then the words are entirely appropriate, in some such form as: 'This cup stands for the new relationship between God and man, made possible by my covenant blood.' He was not in the least asking them to drink blood. He was asking them, every time they did this, to remember what he had done and what it had cost to do it. It seems to us that these additions to the simple saying, 'This is my blood', are not only appropriate, but even essential. We would hold that the reference to the Suffering Servant and the reference to the covenant blood are necessary parts of the original words of institution.

[27] C. G. Montefiore, *The Synoptic Gospels*, I, p. 332; H. Loewe, *A Rabbinic Anthology*, p. 647; cf. J. Klausner, *Jesus of Nazareth*, ET, p. 329, where it is said that it is impossible for Jesus to have invited his disciples to drink his blood. The passages are quoted in A. J. B. Higgins, *The Lord's Supper in the New Testament*, p. 30.

The Word of Repetition

We now come to what appears to be a very definite difference between the words of the institution of the Lord's Supper in Luke and Paul as opposed to Matthew and Mark. Both Luke and Paul have the order to repeat what has been done. Luke has it once, after the bread: 'Do this in remembrance of me'.[28] Paul has it twice, first after the bread, 'Do this in remembrance of me', and second after the cup, 'Do this as often as you drink it in remembrance of me'.[29] The obvious question is, Is this command part of the original words of institution, or is it not? Is it part of the original tradition, or was it added, perhaps by Paul himself, in order to authenticate an already existing practice?

Lietzmann put forward the view that the words were added by Paul, and that they were added because Paul altered the character of the Lord's Supper altogether.[30] There was in the ancient world a custom of funeral banquets, or commemorative meals, or meals of remembrance. They were held not only to commemorate the dead, but also to see that the correct rites were paid to the dead, so that their spirits would be propitious. Epicurus, for instance, left his whole estate to the philosophical school which he had founded with the provisos that the proper sacrifices should be made for his father, mother, brothers, and himself, that out of the income of the estate a birthday celebration should be held on the 10th Gamelion each year, and that on the twentieth day of each month a meeting of the students should be held.[31] An inscription from Nicomedia recalls how someone left an amount of money to a village on condition that they would celebrate his *anamnēsis* (the word of both Paul and Luke) under certain circumstances.[32] In Roman times this became very common indeed. These *in memoriam* meals became very common, but they became in the end more pleasant occasions than anything else. By the second century,

[28] Luke 22.19.   [29] I Corinthians 11.24 f.

[30] H. Lietzmann, *Mass and Lord's Supper*. Lietzmann's position and its developments are summarized in J. Jeremias, *The Eucharistic Words of Jesus*, pp. 238–243.

[31] Diogenes Laertius 10.16.

[32] Quoted in J. Jeremias, *The Eucharistic Words of Jesus*, p. 240.

the Roman Emperors were so suspicious of sedition that practically all clubs and associations were forbidden. When Pliny was governor of Bithynia he transmitted to the Emperor Trajan a request from a group to form a fire-brigade, seemingly a harmless and even a useful request; but such was the fear of clubs and associations that Trajan refused it.[33] In such circumstances, clubs to hold commemorative feasts for the dead were common. There is no doubt at all that these commemorative funeral feasts were held. So, it is suggested, Paul changed the character of the Lord's Supper from being a fellowship meal in which Christians met together, and made it a commemorative meal for the dead on pagan models.

There are certain facts which make this less than likely. In the first place, such meals were held regularly on the anniversary of the *birth*, the birthday, not on the anniversary of the death of the person commemorated. And in the second place, nothing was further from Christian thought than the idea that what was happening in the Lord's Supper was the remembering of a dead man. In any account of the Lord's Supper there is a forward as well as a backward look, an expectation of victorious triumph as well as the memory of a cross. The idea that this command to repeat was added to turn a fellowship meal into a commemorative banquet for the dead does not fit the facts.

Let us for the moment leave the question of the originality of these words, and let us turn to the question of their meaning. 'Do this in remembrance of me.' The ordinary meaning of this phrase, the almost universally accepted meaning, and, we believe, the natural meaning is that Jesus is bidding his disciples repeat this meal in the future, so that the repetition of it will help them to remember, and never to forget, him. Jeremias will have none of this. 'Was Jesus afraid that his disciples would forget him?' he demands, and he expounds his own theory as to the meaning.[34] It is Jeremias' belief that what Jesus is asking for is action designed to make God remember him, and so remembering, bring in the triumph of the Messiah. As Jeremias sees it, Jesus is saying: 'Do this so that God may remember me',

[33] Pliny, *To Trajan*, 10.33, 34.
[34] J. Jeremias, *The Eucharistic Words of Jesus*, pp. 244–255.

D

and for God to remember someone is not simply for God to recall that person to his mind; it is for God to put out his vindicating and triumphant power on behalf of the person he remembers.

What are the grounds for this, and is it a view which must be accepted? *In remembrance of me* is in the Greek *eis tēn emēn anamnēsin*, which literally means *with a view to the remembering of me*. *Anamnēsis* is only very rarely used in the Greek Old Testament.[35] But the word *mnēmosunon* is used about sixty times, and in meaning it is not greatly different. It is the contention of Jeremias that when something is done in the Old Testament for remembering, then the person who is going to do the remembering is God. There is no doubt at all that the idea of putting God in remembrance of someone is an Old Testament idea. Isaiah writes:

> You who put the Lord in remembrance, take no rest,
> and give him no rest
> until he establishes Jerusalem
> and makes it a praise in the earth.[36]

When Aaron (the high priest) goes into the Holy Place, he will wear the breastplate with the stones with the names of the tribes engraved upon them 'to bring them to continual remembrance before the Lord'.[37] The tribute money that the people are to pay is 'to bring the people of Israel to remembrance before the Lord'.[38] The trumpets are to be blown when the offerings are made. 'They shall serve you for remembrance before your God.'[39] Moses and Eleazar bring the gold into the temple, 'as a memorial for the people of Israel before the Lord'.[40] Frequently in regard to offerings the phrase 'the memorial portion' is used,[41] the portion meant to make God remember the offerer in grace and pity. There is no doubt at all that the idea of bringing oneself or others to the remembrance of God is a familiar idea to the Old Testament. We repeat that the idea

---

[35] Leviticus 24.7; Numbers 10.10; in the titles of Psalms 37 and 69; Wisdom 16.6.
[36] Isaiah 62. 6 f.   [37] Exodus 28.29.   [38] Exodus 30.16.
[39] Numbers 10.10.   [40] Numbers 31.54.
[41] Leviticus 2.2, 9; 5.12; 6.15; 24.7; Numbers 5.15, 26.

is not that the person has passed out of God's recollection; the idea is that the person has not yet been the recipient of the action of the gracious power of God, and the hope and prayer is that at last he will become so. On the face of it, there is nothing impossible in the view that Jesus wishes God to remember him with vindicating power.

But there is another side to this, and there are times when the memory to be awakened is definitely and certainly the memory of man. The doom of Amalek is to be written 'as a memorial in a book'.[42] Certain things are to be done as a reminder to the people that the person who is not a priest must not burn incense to the Lord, lest he meet the same fate as Korah and his company.[43] The stones which were taken from the bed of Jordan at the crossing of the river are to be set up 'as a memorial to the people of Israel for ever'.[44] In the story of Esther, certain days are set apart as a memorial of all that happened.[45]

But the passage which really settles the matter is the passage about the Passover in Egypt. We read: 'This day shall be for you a memorial day, and you shall keep it as a feast to the Lord'. And then later there is the instruction that the children must be told the story of what happened. And still later the unleavened bread is a memorial that God brought them out of Egypt.[46] If there is one thing certain, it is that the Passover is a memorial feast to keep for ever green the memory of the miraculous deliverance from Egypt. It was a memorial meal that Jesus used for his purposes; and what could be more natural than that he turned the old memorial of deliverance into a new memorial of what he had done and was about to do? There seems to us no doubt that Jesus was giving men something whereby they might remember him. Linguistically, it is perfectly possible that the phrase could mean that Jesus wanted something done whereby God would remember him, but, when we remember that the whole thing was happening against the background of the Passover, then it is much more natural to take it that it is the memory of man which is in question.

[42] Exodus 17.14. [43] Numbers 16.40. [44] Joshua 4.7.
[45] Esther 9.27 f. [46] Exodus 12.14, 26: 13.7–9.

We take it, then, that the reference in this sentence is to the memory of the disciples in the days to come. We also take it that this sentence does go back to Jesus himself. It is his reorientation of an ancient memorial. The Passover Feast was always a feast which commemorated the saving action of God; and now this saving action is to be demonstrated in a new and unique way. And just as the ancient memory had to be kept sharp and vivid, so had the new memory. Jeremias, we saw, will not accept the possibility that Jesus thought that his disciples might forget. But Jesus knew human nature; he knew how even the most vivid and poignant and heart-searching experience can lose its cutting edge.

> We forget because we must
> And not because we will.

He therefore left this instruction.

But, if so, why does it not appear in the Mark–Matthew tradition, while it does appear in the Paul–Luke tradition? As to this we can only speculate. There are three possible reasons. First, it may have been omitted because one line of the tradition did not think it necessary to insert it, because the repetition of the meal was standard and continuous practice. Second, it may have been omitted because it was not so much part of the ritual of the Lord's Supper as it was instruction about the Supper. Jeremias quotes the saying of Benoit: 'On ne récite pas une rubrique, on l'exécute.'[47] A rubric is not recited, but carried out. This is not so much part of the words of the institution as it is instruction to the Church. Third, and this is another way of saying the same thing, in the Mark–Matthew tradition we may have a liturgical tradition in which only the words of the institution as they affect Jesus are given; in Paul–Luke we have narrative rather than liturgy, and therein the words are perfectly in place. As Jeremias remarks: 'After all, Jesus said more at the Last Supper than the few words preserved in the liturgical formulae.'[48] And this is the additional material.

[47] J. Jeremias, *The Eucharistic Words of Jesus*, p. 238.
[48] J. Jeremias, *op. cit.*, p. 238.

The Saying about the Future

All three Gospels have a saying in which Jesus refers to the future. In Matthew and Mark it comes at the end of the words of institution; in Luke it precedes them.

Truly, I say to you, I shall not drink again of the fruit of the vine until that day when I drink it new in the kingdom of God.[49]

I tell you I shall not drink again of this fruit of the vine until that day when I drink it new with you in my Father's kingdom.[50]

I have earnestly desired to eat this passover with you before I suffer; for I tell you I shall not eat it until it is fulfilled in the kingdom of God.[51]

The eschatological note is struck again in Paul's final comment, although in Paul's version the words are the words of Paul and not of Jesus.

For as often as you eat this bread and drink this cup, you proclaim the Lord's death until he comes.[52]

The variation in the wording is not important, and the place of the saying does not greatly matter. But that this is a genuine and authentic saying of Jesus there is no doubt. It is a saying which is thoroughly in the tradition of Jewish thought. One of the regular features of Jewish thought about the future is the Messianic banquet which God will prepare for his people when he breaks into history, and at which Leviathan and Behemoth will be the food to be eaten.[53]

This idea runs through Jewish thought. It is hinted at in the Old Testament. Zephaniah says: 'For the day of the Lord is at hand; the Lord has prepared a sacrifice and consecrated his guests.'[54] It emerges in the inter-testamental literature. 'Then will the Messiah begin to manifest himself. And Behemoth will show himself from his land, and Leviathan shall ascend from the sea; and these two mighty sea-monsters, whom I created

---

[49] Mark 14.25. [50] Matthew 26.29. [51] Luke 22.15.
[52] I Corinthians 11.26.
[53] Cf. W. O. E. Oesterley, *The Doctrine of the Last Things*, pp. 60 f.; 122–124; 142–144; 187–189.
[54] Zephaniah 1.7.

on the fifth day of the work of Creation and have reserved until that time, shall then be for food for all those who are left.'[55] It is in the Rabbinic literature. There will be a Messianic banquet at which the Israelites will feast on the ox prepared for them from the beginning of the world.[56] At the general resurrection a banquet will be given by God and the flesh of Leviathan eaten.[57] It has its echoes in the New Testament in the saying that many will come from the east and the west and recline with Abraham, Isaac and Jacob in the kingdom of God.[58] It is behind the saying: 'Blessed is he who shall eat bread in the kingdom of God.'[59]

The saying is important, because it shows Jesus' Messianic consciousness and his confidence in final victory. And it is also important, a point to which we shall return, because it shows that the Last Supper had a forward look into the eschatological future. This saying is an integral part of the sayings of Jesus at the Last Supper.

Conclusion

Can we, then, finally come to some conclusion as to the words that Jesus actually used? At first sight, it is surprising that there are so many different versions of them, and later there will be certain conclusions to be drawn from that variation. But when one thinks of it, the variation is natural and inevitable. There was no one taking down a shorthand note of the proceedings at the Lord's Supper. The minds of those who shared in it were baffled and confused and in turmoil, and their hearts were breaking as what was to them the final and incomprehensible tragedy loomed inescapably ahead. Even when they looked back and saw the meal in a sheen of glory, it must still have been wrapped in a haze of bewildered pain. It was an occasion which, when the participants in it looked back, would leave a vivid and poignant memory of feelings and emotions, but in which details would necessarily be blurred. No one who

[55] *Apocalypse of Baruch* 29.3–8.
[56] *Targum of Jonathan* to Numbers ii. 26 ff.
[57] *Baba Bathra* 74a.   [58] Matthew 8.11; Luke 13.29.   [59] Luke 14.15.

truly loved Jesus could ever have given a verbatim account of what happened on that evening.

But the general lines would be, and are, clear. C. H. Turner calls attention to the narrative of the Last Supper in the text of Mark in *k*, Codex Bobiensis, one of the most valuable of the Old Latin manuscripts.[60] Codex Bobiensis was written at Bobbio and is now at Turin. It is said to have belonged to St Columban (543–615). It originally contained the four Gospels, but only Mark 8–16.8 and Matthew 1–15 remains. The manuscript itself is probably fifth or sixth century, but it represents the text used by Cyprian in the middle of the third century. It has a text which is, so to speak, stripped to the bare essentials.

And while they were eating, he took bread, and blessed it, and broke it and gave it to them, and they all ate of it. And he said to them: This is my body. And he took a cup, and blessed it, and gave it to them, and they all drank from it, and he said to them: This is my blood of the covenant which is being shed on behalf of many. Truly I say to you that I will not drink of this fruit of the vine, until that day when I shall drink it new in the Kingdom of God.

Without trying to be certain about every word, we may say that there are four elements in the words of the institution. (i) A statement that the bread is the body of Jesus, and that it was for them. (ii) A statement that the cup represents the covenant blood of the new covenant, that is, the new relationship between man and God, made possible at the cost of the life and death of Jesus. (iii) An instruction to repeat this meal in the days to come, so that the memory of Jesus and what he had done and can do is always fresh. (iv) An eschatological saying in which Jesus affirms his confidence in the full coming of the Kingdom.

[60] C. H. Turner, *St Mark*, p. 68. Codex Bobiensis is transcribed, edited and annotated by J. Wordsworth, *Old Latin Biblical Texts*, vol. 2.

4

DEVELOPMENT OR COMPLICATION?

ONE of the simplest and the oldest acts of fellowship in the world is that of eating together. To share a common meal, especially if the act of sharing the meal also involves the sharing of a common memory, is one of the basic expressions of human fellowship. And it was exactly in this way that the Lord's Supper began. In the modern church the Lord's Supper is not in the physical sense of the term a meal. It is the hunger of the soul and not the hunger of the body that it is now designed to satisfy. But it began from the Passover, a feast of hungry men, who were to clear the table and to leave nothing; and the Lord's Supper began in the Christian Church as a meal in which physical as well as spiritual hunger was satisfied.

The characteristic Jewish phrase for beginning a meal is to break bread. In Acts we read of the early Christians attending the Temple and breaking bread in their homes and partaking of food with glad and generous hearts.[1] We read of the Church at Troas meeting to break bread and eating.[2] The common meal was at the very centre of the Christian fellowship. In I Corinthians[3] we have by implication a description of such a meal. In Corinth it has gone wrong and Paul rebukes the Corinthians for what happened in their fellowship. It should have been a meal of sharing; it should have been a meal at which rich and poor, high and low sat down together in perfect fellowship. In fact, it has become a meal at which some fed to excess and to drunkenness and at which some starved. But the picture is the picture of a real meal, which was the hallmark of a real fellowship.

[1] Acts 2.46.　　[2] Acts 20.7, 11.　　[3] I Corinthians 11.17–22.

This fellowship meal had a name which expresses what it was meant to be. It was called the *agapē*, the Love Feast. The word occurs at least once and perhaps twice in the New Testament. It certainly occurs in the Letter of Jude, which speaks of the heretical members of the fellowship as being 'blemishes on your love feasts'.[4] It may, probably does, occur in the parallel passage in II Peter.[5] There the RSV text speaks of the mistaken Christians 'revelling in their dissipation', but notes in the margin that there is an alternative reading, 'revelling in their love feasts'.[6] Here we have unmistakable proof that the Love Feast did exist in the early days of the Church, and that it was a real meal, so real that it could become a gluttonous and drunken act, bereft both of all religious and community value.

It was, we believe, as this fellowship meal, the Love Feast, that the Lord's Supper began. It would be very much more natural for an act of fellowship to begin as a real meal than for it to begin as a formal ceremony. The word for *Supper* is further proof of this. The word is *deipnon*. It may be that to western ideas the word *Supper* is misleading, for in the west supper is a light meal. But in Greece and in Palestine the *deipnon* was the evening meal, and it was the only main meal of the day. Breakfast was no more than bread taken with water or with diluted wine. The midday meal was likely to be eaten in the street in the open air and not at home at all. It was no more than a picnic snack. The *deipnon* was the evening meal, eaten by the family at home, the one main and principal meal of the day.

The Love Feast lasted for some centuries. Even when the ceremony of the Lord's Supper had been separated from it, for long it still went on. When Ignatius was writing to his churches just before his martyrdom, about AD 110, he wrote to the church at Smyrna:

Let that be considered a valid Eucharist which is celebrated by the

4 Jude 12. 5 II Peter 2.13.
6 The two words are very like each other in Greek. *Dissipations* (it is plural in the Greek) is *apatais*, and *love feasts* is *agapais*. The words could easily be confused.

bishop, or by one whom he appoints. . . . It is not lawful either to baptize or to hold an *agapē* without the bishop.[7]

During the reign of Trajan (AD 98–117), Pliny wrote his famous description of the Christians to the Emperor, describing the situation in Bithynia of which he was governor:

They were in the habit of meeting on a certain fixed day before it was light, when they sang in alternate verses a hymn to Christ, as to a god, and bound themselves by a solemn oath not to commit any wicked deeds, but never to commit any fraud, theft or adultery, nor deny a trust when they should be called upon to deliver it up; after which it was their custom to separate, and then reassemble to partake of food, but food of ordinary and innocent kind.[8]

Here again we have the fellowship meal, and the additional information that it was in the evening.

In AD 197/198 Tertullian wrote his Apology in North Africa, and he too describes the *agapē*, defending it against the heathen slanders of excesses, and comparing it with the immoralities of heathen feasts.

Our dinner shows its idea in its name; it is called by the Greek name for love (*agapē*). Whatever the cost, it is gain to spend in piety's name, for with that refreshment we help the needy. . . . Since it turns on the duty of religion, it allows nothing vile, nothing immodest. We do not take our places at the table until we have first tasted prayer to God. Only so much is eaten as satisfies hunger; only so much drunk as meets the needs of the modest. They satisfy themselves only so far as men who recall that even during the night they must worship God; they talk as those would who know that the Lord listens. After water for the hands come the lights; and then each, from what he knows of the Holy Scriptures, or from his own heart, is called before the rest to sing to God. (The meaning is to prophesy); so that is a test of how much he has drunk. Prayer in like manner ends the banquet. Then we break up; but not to form groups for violence nor gangs for disorder, nor outbursts of lust; but to pursue the same care for self-control and chastity, as men who have dined not so much on dinner as on discipline.[9]

[7] Ignatius, *To the Smyrnaeans* 8.1.   [8] Pliny, *Letters* 10.96.
[9] Tertullian, *Apology* 39.16–19. The translation is that of T. R. Glover in the *Loeb Classical Library*.

About the same time, perhaps about AD 210, Minucius Felix wrote in his *Octavius*:

Our feasts are conducted not only with modesty, but in sobriety; for we do not indulge in delicacies, or prolong conviviality with wine; but temper our gaiety with gravity, with chaste conversation.[10]

We learn from Origen that towards the end of the second century Celsus calumniates the *agapē*.[11] Cyprian speaks of 'the temperate meal resounding with psalms'.[12] There are careful regulations for the *agapē* in Hippolytus' *Treatise on the Apostolic Tradition*. The bishop is there and the people are exhorted and the poor are remembered.

But when you eat and drink, do it in good order and not unto drunkenness, and not so that anyone may mock you, or that he who invites you may be grieved by your disorder, but rather that he may pray to be made worthy that the saints may come in unto him. . . . But if you are invited all to eat together, eat sufficiently, but so that there may remain something over that your host may send it to whomsoever he wills as the superfluity of the saints, and he to whom it is sent may rejoice with what is left over. And let the guests when they eat partake in silence without arguing. But let them listen to any exhortation the bishop may make, and if anyone ask any question, let an answer be given him.[13]

One of the most interesting forms of the *agapē* is that which Charles Bigg distinguished in Clement of Alexandria (c. AD 150–213). In Alexandria there were two kinds of *agapē*, one public and the other private, and as yet the Lord's Supper had not been separated from the *agapē*. The private *agapē* was in fact nothing other than the household meal. Bigg writes of what Clement says:

But of all his phrases the most important are those which assure us that the ordinary meal of a Christian household was in a real sense an *agapē*. It was preceded by the same acts of worship; it was blessed by thanksgiving; it was a true Eucharist. The house father is

[10] Minucius Felix, *Octavius* 31.5. The translation is that of T. R. Glover in the *Loeb Classical Library*.
[11] Origen, *Against Celsus* 1.1.   [12] Cyprian, *To Donatus* 16.
[13] Hippolytus, *The Apostolic Tradition* 26. The translation is from vol. I of the edition of Gregory Dix.

the house priest. The highest act of Christian devotion is at the same time the simplest and the most natural. Husband, wife and child, the house slave and the invited guest gathered round the domestic board to enjoy with thankfulness the good gifts of God, uplifting their hearts in filial devotion, expanding them in brotherly bounty and kindness. To us the word Eucharist has become a term of ritual, whose proper meaning is all but obsolete. To the Greek it was still a word of common life – thanksgiving, the grateful sense of benefits received, of good gifts showered by the good Father on mind and heart and body. '*He that eateth and drinketh unto the Lord* and (*giveth*) *God thanks*' (Romans 14.6) . . . so that a religious meal is an Eucharist.[14]

At this stage the *agapē*, the Lord's Supper, and the family meal are all interwoven and intertwined.

As time went on the *agapē* began to change. It becomes separated from the sacrament of the Lord's Supper, and in the first place it became a kind of charity meal, by the third or fourth century. In the *Didascalia* it has become a meal for old women. In Chrysostom it has become a meal which the rich provide after the sacrament.[15] In Augustine it has become a charity supper.[16]

But the days of the *agapē* were numbered. In the middle of the fourth century its place is in debate. The Council of Laodicea forbade it within churches, but the Synod of Gangra still kept it. The Synod of Hippo in AD 393 and of Carthage in AD 397 both insisted on fasting communion, which may well have been aimed at the complete separation of the *agapē* and the Eucharist, and finally the Trullan Council of AD 692 prohibited it altogether.

Why should this have happened to the *agapē*? Why should it have first been separated from the Eucharist and finally dropped from the life of the Church altogether? The answer is in the New Testament itself. The *agapē* was peculiarly liable to abuse.[17] What should have been a feast of fellowship could become a feast at which snobbish social distinctions wrecked

---

[14] Clement of Alexandria, *Paedagogus* 2.1.10. C. Bigg, *The Christian Platonists of Alexandria*, pp. 139 f.
[15] Chrysostom, *Homily* 22.   [16] Augustine, *C. Faust.* 20.20.
[17] I Corinthians 11.17–22; Jude 12; II Peter 2.13.

fellowship. What should have been a chaste and temperate meal could degenerate into an occasion for drunkenness and gluttony. And this was even more so when people were flooding into the Church from a pagan background, and with no knowledge of anything other than pagan social occasions. There were places in the West when even by the middle of the second century the *agapē* and the Eucharist were separated, for Justin Martyr in his description of a church service has no mention of the *agapē* at all.[18] Already in I Corinthians it is clear that an *agapē* could tear the congregation apart rather than join it in fellowship. The very insistence of the early writers on the chaste innocence of the *agapē* shows the underlying danger. The very condemnation of gluttonous and drunken indulgence shows how real the peril was. Clement of Alexandria writes:

They dare to apply the name *agapē* to pitiful suppers redolent of savour and sauces. They dishonour the good and saving work of the Word, the consecrated *agapē*, with pots and pouring of sauce, and by drink and delicacies and smoke they desecrate that name . . . Such entertainments the Lord has not called *agapae*.[19]

The *agapē* became a casualty because human nature debased a lovely thing until it became a handicap rather than a help to the Christian fellowship – and it is one of the tragedies of the life of the Church that it should have been so.

We now turn to the development which took place in the conception of the Eucharist itself. The development turns on two questions. First, how is the presence of Christ in the Eucharist to be thought of, and in particular what does it mean to say that the bread is his body and the cup is his blood? Second, are we to say that Christ's sacrifice is remembered, or repeated, in the Eucharist? It is obvious that we can only take a panoramic view of this development and that we cannot enter into the details of it. When we do so, we shall find that there is a steady development in which the language of devotion turns into the language of theology, and in which that which had

[18] Justin Martyr, *First Apology* 67.
[19] Clement of Alexandria, *Paedagogus* 2.

once been left undefined was more and more rigidly defined. At the moment we shall start beyond the New Testament, so that after we have traced the lines of the development we can set them against the New Testament. The period from the Apostolic Fathers to the Reformation falls into five sections.

First, here is the earliest period. At the beginning we find Ignatius. Ignatius can speak freely about the bread and the wine being the body and the blood of Jesus Christ. There is one Eucharist, for there is one flesh of our Lord Jesus Christ and one cup for union with his blood.[20] The heretics do not confess that the Eucharist is the flesh of our Saviour Jesus Christ who suffered for our sins.[21] This eucharistic bread is 'the medicine of immortality, the antidote that we should not die, but live for ever in Jesus Christ'.[22] If a man is not within the sanctuary he lacks the bread of God.[23] The Gospel is his refuge as the flesh of Jesus Christ.[24] But just how far Ignatius is from literalizing all this can be seen in the way in which he spiritualizes the whole idea. He speaks about how the things of earth have no attraction for him:

I desire the bread of God, which is the flesh of Jesus Christ, who was of the seed of David, and for drink I desire his blood, which is incorruptible love.[25]

The blood is the symbol of the deathless love of Jesus Christ. He writes to the Trallians:

Be renewed in faith which is the flesh of the Lord, and in love which is the blood of Jesus Christ.[26]

It is clear that Ignatius has no cut and dried theological theory of how the bread and the wine are the body and the blood of Jesus Christ. They are for him the symbols of love and faith and the food of life eternal.

Next within this period there is Justin Martyr. With Justin Martyr there is an advance. The bread and wine are not

---

[20] Ignatius, *To the Philadelphians* 4. [21] Ignatius, *To the Smyrnaeans* 7.
[22] Ignatius, *To the Ephesians* 20. [23] Ignatius, *To the Ephesians* 5.
[24] Ignatius, *To the Philadelphians* 5. This may be a reference to the full and real humanity of Jesus rather than to the Eucharist.
[25] Ignatius, *To the Romans* 7. [26] Ignatius, *To the Trallians* 8.

received as common bread or common drink. They become Christ's body 'through the prayer of the word which came from him'. This can mean either 'through the prayer which Jesus taught his followers to pray as they remembered him in the Lord's Supper', or 'through the prayer of the Word, that is, through the mediating activity of the Logos'. Just as the word became flesh, so the bread and wine become his body.[27] This is much more developed than Ignatius, but it is still moving in the sphere of devotion rather than in the sphere of theology.

Third in this first period comes Irenaeus. Irenaeus is even more definite and carries the matter even further. The heretics, the Gnostics with their hatred of matter, cannot say that 'the bread over which thanks have been given is the body of their Lord, and the cup his blood'. Our bodies are 'nourished with the body of the Lord and with his blood'. Christ called the bread and the wine his body and his blood.[28] The change comes when the invocation of God is spoken over the bread. It no longer then remains common bread. The consecrated bread has now two realities, an earthly and a heavenly one.[29] The importance of this is that Irenaeus is saying that when the invocation is said over the bread, it acquires something which previously it had not, and spiritually it becomes the body of Christ. Irenaeus is moving to something more definite, but he is still moving within the spiritual world, and it is the needs of devotion with which he is concerned rather than any theological definition.

The second period is the period of the third and fourth centuries. Within this period certain far-reaching developments take place. But before we come to them we must note that in many of the writers of this period there are two kinds of passages. There are passages in which they speak with almost literal crudeness about the bread and the wine being the body and the blood of Jesus Christ, and equally there are passages in which these same writers speak of the bread and wine being the symbols of the body and the blood of Christ. But it is true

[27] Justin Martyr, *First Apology* 65–67.
[28] Irenaeus, *Against Heresies* 4.18.4, 5; 5.2.2.
[29] Ibid. 4.18.5.

that within this period the symbols do tend to become more and more identified with that of which they are symbols. There is, for instance, more and more respect for the bread and wine themselves. They are so. sacred that not a crumb must fall and not a drop be lost.[30] *The Apostolic Tradition* of Hippolytus is very definite:

> And let all take care that no unbaptized person taste of the Eucharist nor a mouse or other animal, and that none of it at all fall and be lost. For it is the Body of Christ to be eaten by them that believe and not to be thought lightly of. For having blessed the cup in the Name of God thou didst receive it as the antitype of the Blood of Christ. Wherefore spill not from it, that no alien spirit lick it up, because thou didst despise it, and become guilty of the Blood of Christ as one who despises the price with which he has been bought.[31]

So the authors of this period can speak of 'handling the Lord's body', and of 'doing violence to the Lord's body'.

These writers can speak most definitely about the bread and wine being the body and the blood of Christ in one breath, and in another speak of them as being symbols. Eusebius of Caesarea talks about the Christian being 'fed with the body of the Saviour'[32] in one place, and in another says that they are the image and symbol of his body and blood.[33] In the Liturgy of Serapion at one time the elements are the body and the blood, at another time they are the likeness (*homoiōma*) of the Lord's body and blood. Basil can speak about partaking of the body and blood of Christ.[34] Chrysostom can speak of eating the body, of burying the teeth in the flesh of Christ, of holding in our hands him who is seated with the Father,[35] phrases than which none could sound more literal, and then he can go on to say that the gift of the sacrament is perceived only with the eyes of the mind and not by the senses.[36]

The care with which we must read phrases which look

[30] Tertullian, *De Corona* 3; *Canons of Hippolytus* 209.
[31] Hippolytus, *The Treatise on the Apostolic Tradition* 32.2, 3, pp. 58 f. in the edition of Gregory Dix.
[32] Eusebius, *De Solemn. Pasch.* 7.   [33] Eusebius, *Dem. Evang.* 8.
[34] Basil, *Letters* 93.
[35] Chrysostom, *Homily on John* 47.1; 46.3; *On the Priesthood* 3.4.
[36] Chrysostom, *Homily on Matthew* 82.4.

literal can be seen in the way the great Alexandrians and their school speak. Origen says that the bread becomes the body of Christ through the word or prayer offered over it.[37] But Clement can regard this eating of the Lord's body and partaking of his blood as meaning sharing in the Lord's incorruptibility, or apprehending his power and essence.[38] Origen can take eating and drinking the body and the blood to signify receiving the teaching and words of Jesus Christ which bring life and so nourish and sustain the soul.[39] Eusebius in expounding John 6.51, 52 says that the flesh and the blood stand for the words and sermons of Jesus.[40]

The simple fact is that it is never safe to try to hold a passionate preacher to the letter of a sermon, and these preachers did say things which in other writings they show to be dramatic and pictorial far more than literal and theological.

But granted all that we have said about the necessity of not taking the words of the writers of this period with too much literalness, there are two figures within it who are of immense importance.

First, in the East there was Cyril of Jerusalem who about AD 347 delivered the famous *Catechetical Lectures*, the *Mystagogical Catecheses*.[41] Cyril introduces something new and far-reaching. He quotes the Pauline warrant[42] and then goes on to say:

Since he himself has declared and said of the bread, *This is my body*, who shall dare to doubt any longer? And since he has affirmed and said, *This is my blood*, who shall ever hesitate, saying, that it is not his blood?

Cyril then goes on to cite the changing of the water into wine at Cana of Galilee.[43] If Jesus could do that, is it then incredible that he should change wine into blood? 'With the fullest assurance,' he says, 'let us partake as of the Body and Blood of

[37] Origen, *Against Celsus* 8.33.
[38] Clement of Alexandria, *Paedagogus* 2.2.19; *Stromateis* 5.10.67.
[39] Origen, *Homily on Matthew* 85.   [40] Eusebius, *Eccles. Theol.* 3.12.
[41] The material in Cyril can conveniently be found in F. L. Cross: *St Cyril of Jerusalem's Lectures on the Christian Sacraments*, No. 51 in the S.P.C.K. series of *Texts for Students*.
[42] I Corinthians 11.23–25.   [43] John 2.1–11.

E

Christ.' He concludes this lecture by urging the catechumens to be fully persuaded 'that what seems bread is not bread, though bread by taste, but the body of Christ; and that what seems wine is not wine, though the taste will have it so, but the blood of Christ'.[44] Before the sacramental elements are eaten, 'we call upon the merciful God to send forth his Holy Spirit upon the gifts lying before him, that he may make the bread the body of Christ, and the wine the blood of Christ, for whatsoever the Holy Spirit has touched is sanctified and changed.'[45] This is to say that the consecration of elements turns them into the body and blood of Christ. The worshipper then partakes of the body of Christ and the cup of his blood. He must take the greatest care not to lose any of it. What care a man would take of a handful of gold dust! And this is more precious than gold or precious stones.[46] It remains to say that, however literal this sounds, there is still need of something in the worshipper. The worshipper is invited to taste and see that God is good.[47] 'Trust not the decision to thy bodily palate; no, but to faith unfaltering; for when we taste, we are bidden to taste, not bread and wine, but the sign of the body and blood of Christ.'[48]

The importance of Cyril is that for him the act of consecration wrought a change in the very nature of the elements, so that they are changed and transformed into the body and blood of Christ, although the need of faith in the worshipper is still real.

The second important figure is Ambrose in the West who became Bishop of Milan in AD 374, and the important document is the treatise *On the Mysteries*, the authenticity of which is questioned. He speaks of eating the body and the flesh of Christ.[49] He goes on to answer the question: 'I see something else, how is it that you assert that I receive the body of Christ?' The answer is:

This is not what nature made, but what the blessing consecrated,

---

[44] *The Mystagogical Catecheses* 4.1, 2, 3, 9.
[45] *The Mystagogical Catecheses* 5.7. The word for *changed* is *metaballesthai*, transformed.
[46] *The Mystagogical Catecheses* 5.21.   [47] Psalm 34.8.
[48] *The Mystagogical Catecheses* 5.20.   [49] *On the Mysteries* 8.48, 49.

and the power of blessing is greater than that of nature, because by blessing nature itself is changed.

He then goes on to prove that grace has more power than nature, and that grace can alter things, as in modern language we might say, supernaturally. Moses' rod changed into a serpent and the serpent back into a rod. The water of the streams of Egypt turned to blood. The waters of the Red Sea turned into solid walls. Elisha made the axe head float contrary to nature.[50] And these alterations are the work of men. How much more can grace change things, if the operator is Jesus Christ? In his creating work he can make things out of nothing. Surely then he can change things which already exist? The Virgin Birth shows how grace can change nature. It is at the consecration that this change is made:

The Lord Jesus himself proclaims, This is my body. Before the blessing of the heavenly words another nature is spoken of, after the consecration the body is signified. He himself speaks of his blood. Before the consecration it has another name, after it is called blood.[51]

So in the treatise *On the Christian Faith* he speaks of the sacramental elements which 'by the mysterious efficacy of holy prayer are transformed into the flesh and the blood'.[52]

It is true that Ambrose still insists that this is spiritual and not bodily food,[53] but something has happened with the conception that at the consecration there is a change in the very nature of the elements, so that beyond nature they have become the body and the blood of Christ. The idea of the conversion and the transformation of the elements introduces a new epoch.

It is clear that this idea of the conversion of the elements would soon raise the question of how it all happened. Gregory of Nyssa, about AD 395, produced an explanation. In the days of Jesus' life on earth bread and wine became his body by the

---

[50] Exodus 4.3 f.; Exodus 7.20 ff.; Exodus 14.21 ff.; II Kings 6.1 ff.
[51] *On the Mysteries* 9.50–54.   [52] *On the Christian Faith* 4.10.125.
[53] *On the Mysteries* 9.58.

natural process of digestion. In the Eucharist they immediately become his body by the action of the Logos.[54]

The next period is the period between the fifth and the eighth centuries. Within this period two conceptions compete. There is the conversion conception, according to which the elements change their nature and are transformed into the actual body and blood of Jesus Christ. And there is the dyophysite, or two-nature, view in which there is a clear distinction between the elements and the realities which they signify, and in which the elements thus have two natures, a physical nature in which they remain bread and wine, and a spiritual nature in which they become the body and blood of the Lord; and it may be said that faith is the connecting link by which the one nature is changed into the other.

In the East it was the conversion conception which triumphed. By the time of John of Damascus, about AD 750, the view is that, once the elements have been consecrated, they become identical with the body and the blood of Jesus Christ. John of Damascus argues that just as in the beginning God made all things by the energy of the Holy Spirit, so now the energy of that same Spirit 'performs those things which are supernatural, and which it is not possible to comprehend, unless by faith alone'. 'The bread itself and wine are changed into God's body and blood.' All that we need to know is that this is done 'by the invocation and presence of the Holy Spirit'. 'The bread and wine are not merely figures of the body and the blood of Christ (God forbid!) but the deified body of the Lord itself.' 'Jesus did not say, "This is a figure of my body"; he said, "This is my body."' 'Let us then receive the body of the crucified One.' Before the act of consecration the bread and the wine are antitypes of the body and the blood of Jesus Christ; after the act of consecration they *are* his body and his blood.[55] And that body of Christ which is received in the Eucharist is none other than the historical body of Christ.

So then in the East the conversion conception of the Eucharist was dominant. But it was not so in the West at this

---

[54] Gregory of Nyssa, *Catechetical Oration* 37.
[55] John of Damascus, *Concerning the Orthodox Faith* 4.13.

period, mainly because the view of Augustine was strongly dyophysite.[56] Augustine had a distinctive view of what a sacrament is. It is 'a visible sign of an invisible thing', and what is honoured in it is not the sign but the thing.[57] One thing is seen, while another thing is understood, and the spiritual benefit is in what is understood, and not in what is seen.[58] There is a clear distinction between the *sacramentum*, the outward part, and the *res sacramenti*, the thing itself,[59] and between the *sacramentum* and the *virtus*, the power, of the *sacramentum*.[60] A sacrament is a visible word.[61]

The clear result of this is that it gives faith in the worshipper a paramount place. 'It is not that which is seen that feeds, but that which is believed.'[62] 'Believe and you have eaten.'[63] The passages in John which speak of eating the flesh of Christ mean to dwell in Christ and to have Christ dwelling in us.

For all this, the elements are not only signs. They are the conveyors of life, but the eating and drinking is a spiritual process, and the life and gift a spiritual life and gift.[64] It is not the physical and the historical body of Christ that we receive in the sacrament. It is the Spirit which quickens it. It is the essence of his humanity in a new and symbolic body.[65] It is therefore only those who dwell in Christ who in the sacrament receive Christ.[66]

The West was not to stop here, although it may well be said that the West was to return here. For the East the consecration of the elements converted them into the literal body and blood of Christ; for Augustine it turned them into 'a sacrament of commemoration of Christ's sacrifice', whose full benefit came only to faith.[67]

---

[56] There is an excellent summary of Augustine's position in J. Hastings, *Encyclopaedia of Religion and Ethics*, in the article on the Eucharist by J. H. Srawley, vol. 5, p. 554. In what follows I have drawn upon that summary.
[57] Augustine, *De Cat. Rud.* 26.50.   [58] Augustine, *Sermon* 272.
[59] Augustine, *Tract. in Joann.* 26.15.
[60] Augustine, *Tract. in Joann.* 26.11.
[61] Augustine, *Tract. in Joann.* 80.3.   [62] Augustine, *Sermon* 112.5.
[63] Augustine, *Tract. in Joann.* 25.12.   [64] Augustine, *Sermon* 131.1.
[65] Augustine, *Tract. in Joann.* 17.5; 26.15; *Sermon* 227; *Letter* 185.
[66] Augustine, *Tract. in Joann.* 26.18.   [67] Augustine, *C. Faust.* 20.21.

The next period is the period of the Middle Ages and extends from AD 800 to 1500. It was during this period that there emerged the most famous of all conceptions of the presence of Jesus Christ in the elements of the sacrament.

The period opened with the old argument between the conversion and the dyophysite views. Two treatises were written *On the Body and Blood of the Lord* about the year AD 844. The first was by a monk called Paschasius Radbertus. He was a thorough-going conversionist. At the consecration, he held, the elements were changed into the actual historical body of Jesus Christ. 'After consecration, they are nothing else than the body and blood of Christ... and that I may speak more marvellously, to be clearly the very flesh which was born of Mary, and suffered on the cross and rose from the tomb.' How this could happen, and how it could happen continuously and universally, he did not try to explain; it happened simply through the miraculous activity of God. To this an answer was made by another monk called Ratramnus. He held that there was no material change in the elements. Outwardly they are the same as ever; inwardly to the mind they are the figure of the body and blood of the Lord. They are not two substances, first material bread and wine, and then second, the literal body of Christ. They are one substance under two aspects. In the bodily aspect they are bread and wine and remain so; in the spiritual aspect they are the body and blood of Jesus Christ. In their material aspect they feed the body; and in their spiritual aspect they feed the soul. Ratramnus came very near to what is called the 'virtualist' position, that is, the position which holds that there is no real or objective change in the elements, but that after their consecration they become spiritually the body and the blood of Jesus Christ, to the man who receives them and partakes of them in faith.

The argument was to flare up again in 1050. At that time Berengar of Tours taught the same doctrine as Ratramnus, which he attributed to John the Scot, that is, Scotus Erigena. He was found guilty of heresy and he was compelled to assent to a statement by Pope Nicholas the Second, which was couched in almost completely physical terms. It stated that, the bread and wine placed on the altar are after consecration not only a sacrament but also the true body and blood of our Lord Jesus Christ, and that these are sensibly handled and broken by the hands of the priests and crushed by the teeth of the faithful, not only sacramentally but in reality.

Berengar after a time resumed his teaching and once again he was condemned by Pope Gregory the Seventh, and required to agree that the elements underwent a *substantial* change into 'the real flesh of Christ which was born of the Virgin. . . .'[68]

Here, then, at the beginning of the Middle Ages, there is still the unsolved problem of what really happens or does not happen to the elements of the sacrament in their relationship to the body of Jesus Christ.

Christian thought in this period was moving to a new conception of the sacrament. Hugh of St Victor and Peter Lombard, both about the middle of the twelfth century, add something. For them a sacrament 'does not only signify; it sanctifies'. A sacrament both contains grace and is the cause of grace. But Peter Lombard completely rejected any idea of the breaking of Christ's body in the fraction of the bread.

It is in the first half of the twelfth century that we first come upon the word which was to be such a battle-ground, for it is then that we first find the word *transubstantiation*. The noun first appears in Hildebert of Tours and the verb in Stephen of Autun. Just what did transubstantiation teach and say?

Transubstantiation was a conception which was the product of the Schoolmen of the twelfth century. There are two separate parts in anything. There is its *substantia*. The *substantia* is the invisible and impalpable universal which inheres in every particular which is included under it. There are the *accidentia*. The *accidentia* are the sensible and visible properties which come into existence when the form or the universal clothes itself in matter.[69] The conception is not unlike the Platonic

[68] For a summary of the positions of Radbertus, Ratramnus and Berengar see Henry Bettenson, *Documents of the Christian Church*, pp. 205-207.

[69] H. Rashdall, *Universities of Europe in the Middle Ages*, pp. 46 f., quoted in J. Hastings, *Encyclopaedia of Religion and Ethics*, vol. 5, p. 558.

doctrine of forms or ideas, the universals of which everything on earth is only a pale and imperfect copy. To take a very simple example, all flowers have the substance of a flower, but different kinds of flowers have the varying forms, the varying *accidentia*, which come when the universal idea of a flower becomes material and sensible in a particular flower.

So, then, the idea of transubstantiation is that in the consecration of the elements the *substantia* change but the *accidentia* remain the same. The *substantia* of the bread and wine become the *substantia* of the body and blood of Christ. The *accidentia* remain the same, and the *accidentia* are all that remain of the original bread and wine. The Fourth Lateran Council in 1215 said: 'His body and blood are really contained in the Sacrament of the altar under the species of bread and wine, the bread being transubstantiated into the Body, and the wine into the Blood, by the power of God.'

The transubstantiation position is made clear by Thomas Aquinas (1225–1274). He denies that the substances of the bread and wine remain after consecration. This would destroy the reality of the sacrament. For the demand is that in it 'there should be the true body of Christ, which was not there before consecration'. A thing cannot be in a place where it was not before unless it is either brought in from some other place or unless by an act of conversion something is changed into it. Now clearly, since Christ is omnipresent, he does not begin to be in the sacrament because his body was brought in from some other place. Therefore Christ can only come into the sacrament by the conversion of the substance of the bread and wine into his body. And when a thing is converted into something else, nothing remains of it; therefore nothing remains of the substance of the bread and wine (*Summa Theologica* 3. Q.65, Art. 2).

Further, this conversion is not like a natural conversion; it is wholly supernatural and due to the power of God. Natural conversion, working according to the laws of nature, can produce no more than a change of form. Only God can produce a conversion in which the whole substance of A becomes the whole substance of B. This is what happens in the sacrament.

By the power of God the whole substance of the bread is converted into the whole substance of Christ's body. 'Hence this conversion is properly called transubstantiation' (*Summa Theologica* 3. Q.65, Art. 4).

But although the substance is converted, the *accidentia*, the outward and material appearance, of the bread and wine remain the same, and for three reasons. First, it is abhorrent for men to eat flesh and drink blood. Therefore the body and the blood are set before us under the appearance of normal and natural food. Second, this happens 'lest this sacrament should be mocked at by the infidels, if we ate our Lord under his proper appearance.' Third, the fact that we take the body and blood 'invisibly' necessitates the taking of them with faith.

Transubstantiation became the orthodox doctrine of the Church in the Middle Ages, and of the whole Church of the West up to the Reformation. The Council of Trent gave the matter its official expression (Section D, *On the Eucharist*, Chapter 4, *On Transubstantiation*):

Since Christ our Redeemer said that that which he offered under the appearance of bread was truly his body, it has therefore always been held in the Church of God, and now this holy Synod declares anew, that through consecration of the bread and wine there comes about a conversion of the whole substance of the bread into the substance of the body of Christ our Lord, and of the whole substance of the wine into the substance of his blood. And this conversion is by the Holy Catholic Church conveniently and properly called transubstantiation.

There follows (chapter 5) the section *On the Worship and Veneration of the Holy Eucharist*:

And so no place is left for doubting that all Christ's faithful should in their veneration display towards this most Holy Sacrament the full worship of adoration (*latriae cultum*) which is due to the true God, in accordance with the custom always received in the Catholic Church. For it is not the less to be adored because it was instituted by Christ the Lord that it might be taken and eaten.

Certain things followed from this. The priest simply by virtue of his ordination and apart altogether from his spiritual or moral quality was able to effect this change in the elements, which makes it a matter of magic rather than of religion. Into this there comes the conception of intention. That which was intended happens. Therefore, if the priest intended the sacrament for all, all receive it, irrespective of their faith or their life or their spiritual condition. The grace of God operates mechanically in the sacrament for all who share in it. The idea that the elements change their substance and become the very substance of the body and the blood of Christ makes the moment of consecration the most important moment in the whole sacramental service, and it begets an adoration and veneration of the elements themselves, which is not far short of idolatry. The very sacredness of the elements after this change makes the taking of communion infrequent and did much to bring about the withholding of the cup from the laity. This was the situation when the Reformation came to Europe.

With the Reformation there come three great figures at whose views we must look.[70] The first of them is Luther.

Two initial things have always to be remembered about Martin Luther. First, the thing which dominates him is the need of a wounded conscience. To him this is not a matter of academic interest and theological argument; it is a matter of the grace of God for a man who is sorely conscious of his sin. The second thing is closely allied to this. Luther is not a natural theologian who by training and custom and instinct weighs and carefully chooses his words. He is a natural preacher who uses vivid and dramatic and often exaggerated language, and it is always to be remembered that often he is speaking as the passionate preacher and not as the careful theologian. Cautious prudence of expression was something unknown to Luther.

Luther had his own distinctive view of what a sacrament is. To him it was not the sacrament which set a man right with God; it was the faith which a man took to the sacrament and drew from the sacrament. The Schoolmen and Aquinas had

[70] There is a good account of the views of Luther, Zwingli and Calvin in J. Hastings, *Encyclopaedia of Religion and Ethics*, article on the Eucharist, vol. 5, pp. 564–569. That section of the article is by Hugh Watt, and it is from it that I have drawn most of the quotations used.

said that the sacraments are effective signs of grace. Luther
agreed, but with one addition – 'if you believe, and not other-
wise'. Luther aimed perhaps above all to restore the Word to
what he believed was its rightful place. A Church based on a
magical view of the sacraments in which the Word has no place
at all was not to Luther a Church. He would indeed have said
that there is in the end only one sacrament, the Sacrament of
the Word.

Luther had to think out his own position in contest with
Andrew Bodenstein of Carlstadt. For Bodenstein the Lord's
Supper was not the sign and seal which gave certainty of
reconciliation. For him it was an act of remembrance which
exercised a moral influence on the mind. It was not for him
basically different from any sermon or any picture which
brought Christ and his sacrifice and his benefits vividly and
piercingly to the mind. It was Bodenstein's contention that
when Jesus said, 'This is my body', he was neither pointing to
nor referring to the bread at all, but simply to his own body,
and that therefore the words in no way identify the bread with
the body of our Lord.

To Luther this was not enough. The main deficiency in it
was that it made everything depend on a subjective experience.
There is no objective pledge and guarantee of the grace of God.
Luther therefore insisted that the words, 'This is my body',
must be accepted in a real way. The aim of the sacrament is
not simply to beget a subjective experience moved by an
awakened memory; it is to provide assurance of salvation by
an objective reality within the sacrament. Of this Luther could
speak with violence. 'Though infinite myriads of devils and all
fanatics should impudently demand how bread and wine can
be the body and blood of Christ, I know that all spirits and
learned men put together have not as much intelligence as
Almighty God has in his little finger.' Two quotations will
show how the violence of Luther's language has to be toned
down. He wrote to Melanchthon in 1534:

In brief, this is our doctrine, that the body of Christ is truly eaten
in and with the bread, so that what the bread does and suffers the

body of Christ does and suffers; it is distributed, eaten, and masticated with the teeth, because of the sacramental union.

But in the Formula of Concord it is much more soberly said:

We also utterly reject and condemn the Capernaitic manducation of the body of Christ . . . as if, forsooth, we taught that the body of Christ is torn by teeth.

There were times when Luther spoke with vivid and dramatic and hyperbolic emphasis because he was so intent on keeping the objective guarantee of the grace of God.

But the question arises, How is this presence of Jesus Christ in the sacrament to be conceived and explained? Luther has two explanations. The first of them was presented to him by the arguments of his critics. They said: 'Scripture says that Jesus Christ is at the right hand of God. How then can he be in the bread and wine of the sacrament?' Luther's answer was that God's right hand is not in a local position, like, for instance, a golden chair. God's right hand is *everywhere*. Therefore, Jesus Christ is everywhere. Therefore, he is in the bread and wine of the sacrament. Luther's other argument came from his doctrine of the *communicatio idiomatum*, the communication of personal attributes. In Jesus Christ, so he argued, there are two natures, and each nature shares in the attributes of the other. They as it were communicate their attributes to each other. If that is so, then the human body of Christ possesses the divine attribute of omnipresence.Therefore, his body is everywhere. Therefore, it is in the elements of the sacrament.

But there is a very real sense in which both these arguments prove too much. They both prove that Jesus Christ is *everywhere*. How then can he be specially present in the elements of the sacrament? Luther's answer is that it is one thing for Jesus Christ to be present; it is another thing for him to be present *for us*. So Luther argues that in the sacrament, 'He is there for you, when he binds himself by his word, and says, "Here you are to find me" '.

For Luther the presence of Jesus Christ in the sacrament was very real. But his presence was not the outcome of any priestly miracle of consecration. When Jesus said in the Upper Room, 'This is my body', the unity of himself and the bread and wine were then and there established, long before any priestly consecration takes place. The unity is there already by the act of God in Christ.

The second of the great Reformation figures is Zwingli. Zwingli differs from Luther in that he never knew the intense desire for grace of the wounded conscience in the way that Luther did. He was not primarily a theologian; he was rather a thinking and educated layman, impatient of what he would have called the priestly manufacture of deity. He came at the Lord's Supper in a different way.

First, Zwingli stressed the community far more and the individual far less than Luther did. For Zwingli the sacrament was a demonstration of, and a way towards, the unity of those who are in the new covenant, and a pledge to live life according to that covenant obligation. 'We eat this bread,' he wrote to Alber, 'that we may become one bread.' For Zwingli this is the sacrament of unity.

Second, Zwingli stressed remembrance. The sacrament is the remembrance of a sacrifice made once and for all, never to be repeated, never needing to be repeated. To share in the benefits of that sacrifice was something that Zwingli greatly desired; to repeat that sacrifice was something that he regarded as impossible. For him the sacrament is rather a remembrance of the crucified Christ.

Third, for Zwingli faith was all-important and his faith was based on the thought of John. He made much of John 6. In that chapter there is repeated mention of eating the flesh of Christ:

Unless you eat the flesh of the Son of Man and drink his blood, you have no life in you; he who eats my flesh and drinks my blood has eternal life, and I will raise him up at the last day. For my flesh is food indeed, and my blood is drink indeed. He who eats my flesh and drinks my blood abides in me, and I in him. As the living Father sent me, and I live because of the Father, so he who eats me will live because of me.[71]

[71] John 6.53–57; cf. John 6.41, 48, 51.

From this Zwingli argued that such eating and drinking has nothing to do with the mouth. Faith is the instrument of reception. And for Zwingli faith includes and indeed is this mystical union in which the believer abides in Christ, and Christ in him. It is in this way that Christ is encountered in the sacrament. Now clearly in the world the closeness and the intimacy and the intensity of this faith varies. If it is to survive, it must be continually renewed by God. In the sacrament we renew this union with Christ; and this is the sense in which he gives himself as our food.

So, then, for Zwingli the sacrament creates union with each other, and renews union with Christ, and it does both by bringing to our remembrance, through the signs of the bread and the wine, the death and sacrifice of Christ.

Zwingli therefore could never bring himself to take 'This is my body' literally. In 1522 he found Gerhard Hoen's interpretation in which the *est* is taken to mean *significat*, signifies, represents. 'This signifies my body.' He found no difficulty in finding parallels to the use of *is* meaning *represents*. In Pharaoh's dream and its interpretation, 'The seven good cows are seven years', the *are* is obviously *represent*.[72] In I Corinthians, 'The Rock was Christ' clearly means, 'The Rock signifies Christ'.[73] For long he searched for an absolutely conclusive parallel and finally in a dream such a parallel came to him – 'It is the Lord's passover', where the *is* clearly means *represents, signifies*.[74]

For Zwingli, the Lord's Supper is a memorial in which we find through the remembrance stimulated by the signs of the bread and wine closer union with each other and renewed union with Christ.

The third of the great Reformation figures was John Calvin. Calvin could not go the whole way with either Luther or Zwingli. He could not accept Luther's scholastic proofs that the body of Christ was everywhere; and he had too intense a sense of religious devotion to accept the view of Zwingli that the bread and wine were no more than signs. He did hold that

[72] Genesis 41.25–27.　　　[73] I Corinthians 10.4.
[74] Exodus 12.11.

in the Lord's Supper we do not only remember Christ; we also receive Christ.

Calvin, too, had his interpretation of the saying that Christ is at the right hand of God. Zwingli had argued that, if Christ is at the right hand of God, he cannot be in the bread and the wine. Luther had argued that, if Christ is at the right hand of God, then he is everywhere, because God's right hand is everywhere, and therefore is in the bread and the wine. But Calvin held that to say that Christ is at the right hand of God is to say that he shares in the majesty and the omnipotence of God. And, if that is so, 'he can pour out his virtue upon us wherever he likes in heaven or in earth'.[75] From him 'there streams a radiance and a power' even above the ordinary influence of the Spirit, and of that radiance and power the worshipper in the sacrament receives. The body of Christ is not anywhere on earth in material substance; it is present in this virtue and power. Christ is present, and being present in power is present with all his gifts to offer. It is not the bread that brings Christ to us; the bread is no more than a 'dead creature'; it is Christ himself who through his Spirit brings himself to us, and the bread and wine are the pledge and the assurance that that is so.

As Hugh Watt says, Calvin's view of the sacrament is dynamical rather than mystical,[76] for in it there is the radiant dynamic virtue and power of Christ available with all his benefits to the worshipper in faith.

Calvin's position is seen quite clearly in his definition of a sacrament and in his view of how the sacrament becomes efficacious. His definition runs thus:

An external symbol by which the Lord attests in our consciences his promises of good will towards us to sustain the inferiority of our faith, and we on our part testify to our piety towards him as well in his presence and before the angels as in the sight of men.[77]

He goes on to write *Concerning the Sacred Supper of Christ*:

That sacred communication of his own flesh and blood by which

[75] John Calvin, *Institutes* 4.17.18.
[76] J. Hastings, *Encyclopaedia of Religion and Ethics*, vol. 5, p. 567.
[77] J. Calvin, *Institutes* 4.14.

Christ pours his own life into us, just as if he were to penetrate into the marrow of our bones, he witnesses and attests in the Supper. And that he does not by putting before us a vain or empty sign, but offering there the efficacy of his Spirit, by which he fulfils his promise. And in truth he offers and displays the thing there signified to all who share that spiritual feast; though only by the faithful is it perceived and its fruits enjoyed.

For Calvin in the sacrament the dynamic action of the Spirit meets the seeking need of man.

We shall for the moment stop there in our investigation, although later we shall go on to look at our present beliefs. We shall now proceed to examine the other great question, and the other great cause of debate, the argument as to whether or not the action of the Lord's Supper constitutes a memorial of a sacrifice or the repetition of that sacrifice. When we were examining the ideas of the connection of the presence of Jesus Christ in the bread and the wine, we had to tread a long road, because there were a large number of possibilities. Some held that there was no connection at all, other than that the bread and the wine were symbols to awaken memory. Some held that from the first moment that Jesus said, 'This is my body', there existed a sacramental connection between the bread and his body and the wine and his blood. Some held that that connection comes into being at the moment of the consecration of the elements. Some held that at that moment of consecration a spiritual identity was created, and that, being a spiritual thing, it needed faith to experience it. Some held that a material identity took place and that after the consecration the elements were identical with the historical body and blood of Jesus, with that body with which he was born, crucified and died. Some held – and this became the orthodox belief of the Roman Catholic Church – that at the moment of consecration there is a change of substance, and the bread and wine cease to have their own substance and become the substance of the body and the blood of Jesus Christ, although they still retain the accidents of bread and wine. It is further clear that the more spiritual the identity is held to be, the greater the need of faith to experience it; and the more material it is held to be, the more it can be experienced by the worshipper, irrespective of what he brings to it.

When we come to discuss whether or not the action of the Lord's Supper constitutes a sacrifice or the commemoration of a sacrifice the way is much less complicated, the development is much clearer, and the answer is much more Yes or No.

In the first period of the Church, with one exception at whom we shall shortly look, none of the writers at all connect the action of the Lord's Supper with propitiatory sacrifice. This is not at all surprising, for it is the conviction of all the early writers that the need for sacrifice is gone, and that the only sacrifice which a Christian can now bring to God is the sacrifice of prayer, of a pure heart, and of an obedient life. For the writer of the Letter of Barnabas the old sacrifices are abolished, 'in order that the new law of our Lord Jesus Christ, which is without the yoke of necessity, might have its oblation not made by man'. We have to be careful not to make the old mistakes of animal sacrifice; the sacrifice desired by God is the contrite heart.[78] In the *Didache* the offering is a thank-offering, and it is only pure when a man has confessed his sins and when he is at peace with his fellowmen.[79] Justin Martyr speaks of Christians all over the world offering sacrifices to God, 'that is the bread of the Eucharist and the cup of the Eucharist'.[80] But he goes on to say that prayers and thanksgivings, when offered by worthy men, are the only perfect and pleasing sacrifice to God, and this is what Christians have undertaken to offer, moved to that offering by the remembrance of the suffering of Christ, which the solid and liquid food of the Eucharist bring.[81] This idea runs all through the early writers. Athenagoras meets the charge of atheism, a charge made because the Christians have neither sacrifices or temples. The noblest sacrifice is to know the God who made the world and who needs no sacrifice. 'Yet it does behove us to offer a bloodless sacrifice, and the service of our reason.'[82] Minucius Felix has a fine passage in

---

[78] *The Letter of Barnabas* 2.4–10.   [79] *Didache* 9, 10, 14.
[80] Justin Martyr, *Dialogue with Trypho* 41.
[81] ibid. 117.
[82] Athenagoras, *Apology* 13; cf. Romans 12.1.

F

which he shows the needlessness of temples and sacrifices and victims to the God in whom the Christians believe:

He who follows after innocence makes prayer to God; he who practises justice offers libations; he who abstains from fraud, propitiates; he who rescues another from peril slays the best victim. These are our sacrifices, these our hallowed rites; with us justice is the true measure of religion.[83]

Irenaeus in a long passage[84] has no difficulty in proving from the prophets that God does not require sacrifices.[85] 'He thus teaches them that God requires obedience, which renders them secure, rather than sacrifices and holocausts, which avail them nothing towards righteousness.' God does not seek sacrifices but faith and obedience. The true incense is the prayers of the saints.[86] In the Eucharist it is a thank-offering we bring for all that redeems and sustains life, and it is a pure sacrifice, for it comes from those who glorify Christ.

With a background of thought like this it is not likely that the idea of propitiatory sacrifice would be prominent. Nor did this ever die out, for in the early part of the fourth century Lactantius is still writing:

He needs not a temple, since the world is his dwelling; he needs not an image, since he is incomprehensible both to the eyes and to the mind; he needs not earthly lights, for he was able to kindle the light of the sun, with the other stars, for the use of man. What then does God require of man but worship of the mind, which is pure and holy?... It is justice only which God requires. In this is sacrifice; in this the worship of God.[87]

But what, apart from a propitiating sacrifice, was participation in the Lord's Supper held to do?

There is a strong and continuous line of thought in which the entry of the body and the blood of Jesus Christ into us is held to work such a change in us that we may be said to be partakers

[83] Minucius Felix, *Octavius* 32.1–3.

[84] Irenaeus, *Against Heresies* 4.17, 18.

[85] I Samuel 15.22; Psalm 40.6; Psalm 51.17; Isaiah 1.11; Jeremiah 6.20; 7.21, 22; 9.24; Zechariah 7.9, 10; 8.16, 17.

[86] Revelation 5.8.

[87] Lactantius, *Institutes* 58, 68, in A. V. G. Allen, *Christian Institutions*, p. 451.

of the divine life and the divine being. We find this first in Ignatius who speaks of, 'breaking one bread, which is the medicine of immortality, the antidote that we should not die, but live for ever in Jesus Christ'.[88] Tertullian speaks of our flesh being fed by the body and blood of Christ, 'that the soul may be sated with God'.[89] Cyril of Jerusalem in his instruction on the Eucharist says that the object of partaking of the body and blood of Christ is .that we might be made 'of the same body and the same blood with him. For thus we come to bear Christ in us, because his body and blood are diffused through our members; thus it is that, according to the blessed Peter, we become partakers of the divine nature.'[90] Hilary thinks in terms of a kind of extension of the incarnation. In the incarnation there happened the union of the Word and flesh, and in the sacrament there happens our union with the Word made flesh.[91] Gregory of Nyssa, startlingly to us, says that in the sacrament Christ infuses himself into our perishable nature so that by communion with the Deity man might be deified. The sacrament, as it has been put, immortalizes our body.[92]

This is startling talk to us, but it was language which the age to which it was addressed could understand, for this is the very language which every Mystery Religion spoke.[93] So, for instance, there are Hermetic papyri which say: 'Enter thou into my spirit and my thoughts my whole life long, for thou art I and I am thou.' 'I know thee, Hermes, and thou knowest me; I am thou, and thou art I.' Through the Mystery Religions, so it was claimed, a man became demortalized. So in the *Liturgy of Mithra* the initiate says: 'I am a man . . . born of mortal womb . . . having this day been begotten again by thee, out of so many myriads rendered immortal in this hour by the goodwill of God in his abounding goodness.' Further, these religions thought in terms of indwelling. 'Come to me,' runs the Hermetic prayer, 'as babes to women's wombs.'

[88] Ignatius, *To the Ephesians* 20.2.
[89] Tertullian, *On the Resurrection of the Flesh* 8.
[90] Cyril of Jerusalem, *The Mystagogical Catecheses* 4.3.
[91] Hilary, *Concerning the Trinity* 8. 13 f.
[92] Gregory, *Catechetical Oration* 37.
[93] Cf. S. Angus, *The Mystery-Religions and Christianity*, pp. 106–112.

When the Christians spoke of the sacrament as infusing divine life into the partaker of it, they spoke the language their hearers knew and understood.

We now come to the definitely sacrificial conception of the Eucharist. We said that of the early writers there was one who stood out as identified with this idea. This was Cyprian. Cyprian deals with this matter in a letter in which he is rebuking those who serve the cup in water instead of wine.[94] Cyprian's main argument is that we must in all things follow the example of Jesus Christ, and in the sacrament the priest must follow Christ's example. Cyprian can speak of offering the cup 'in commemoration of the Lord and his passion',[95] but in the preceding sentence he speaks of the Lord's passion as the sacrifice we offer. The salient passage runs:

If Christ Jesus our Lord and God is himself the high priest of God the Father and first offered himself as a sacrifice to the Father, and commanded this to be done in remembrance of himself, then assuredly the priest acts truly in Christ's room, when he imitates what Christ did, and he offers then a true and complete sacrifice to God the Father, if he so begin to offer as he sees Christ himself has offered.[96]

It is not offering a new sacrifice; it is offering the sacrifice which Christ has already offered, but the course is set for the Eucharist to become a propitiatory offering and sacrifice. Origen takes the shewbread as a parallel. It was an offering to draw God's attention to his people; it was a propitiatory memorial; and so the memorial of Christ has also propitiating power.[97] Eusebius can speak of offering the body of Christ. The sacrament is still a memorial, but it is connected with the sacrificial forgiveness of sins.[98] Still more definite is Cyril of Jerusalem. He speaks of presenting that 'holy and most awful sacrifice', and holds that it is effective for the blessed dead as

---

[94] *Letter* 63, but numbered 62 in the Ante-Nicene Library translation. The most relevant part of the letter is quoted in Henry Bettenson, *Documents of the Christian Church*, p. 108.
[95] *Letter* 63.17.
[96] *Letter* 63.14.
[97] Origen, *Homily on Leviticus* 13.
[98] Eusebius, *The Demonstration of the Gospel* 1.10.

well as for the living. He says that after 'the bloodless service of the sacrifice of propitiation', prayers are made for the peace of the Church.[99] With him the element of propitiation is established. It is in fact the main element in the sacrament.

Even more dramatic is the picture of Chrysostom. He speaks of 'the most awful sacrifice'. He speaks of the Lord sacrificed and lying there, with the priest standing over the sacrifice and praying, 'all reddened with that blood'.[100] It is true that he says that we do not offer a different sacrifice, but always the same, the sacrifice already made once and for all, and, like the writer of the Letter to the Hebrews, he thinks of the whole action as being heavenly action in the spiritual region.[101] This idea of propitiating sacrifice gets into the liturgies. For instance, in the Liturgy of Serapion there is the prayer: 'We beseech thee through this sacrifice be reconciled to all of us and be merciful.'

As usual, Augustine deals judiciously with this. For him the Eucharist is 'a commemoration of the sacrifice on the Cross'.[102] The sacrifice was prefigured in the Old Testament, offered on Calvary, and celebrated in the Eucharist.[103] But he too can speak of offering the body of Christ. He has the special idea and the beautiful idea that in the Eucharist the faithful achieve such a union with Christ that they become the body of Christ, and sacrifice themselves.[104]

In the sixth century Gregory the Great says that in a mystery the Eucharist renews (*reparat*) the sacrifice of Christ. It imitates the passion of the only-begotten Son. But like Chrysostom he sees the action in heaven. 'He who is immolated for us again in the mystery of the holy oblation is the Son who dies no more, but lives in himself immortally and incorruptibly. In the Eucharist things earthly are united with things heavenly.' Like Augustine, Gregory has the idea of the involvement of those who partake. The sacrifice is consummated in their

[99] Cyril of Jerusalem, *Mystagogical Catecheses* 4.8, 9.
[100] Chrysostom, *On the Priesthood* 3.4'; cf. the comments in J. A. Nairn's edition in *Cambridge Patristic Texts*.
[101] Chrysostom, *Homily* 12.3; 14.1, 2; 17.3.
[102] Augustine, *C. Faust.* 20.18, 21.
[103] Augustine, *C. Faust.* 20.21.
[104] Augustine, *Sermon* 227; *City of God* 10.6.

self-offering. 'For thus will he be totally the victim for us to God, when we have made ourselves a victim.'[105]

During the later Middle Ages the connection of the Lord's Supper with propitiatory sacrifice was not something which was discussed. The Schoolmen were too concerned with the discussion of the way in which Christ was present in the sacrament to give much thought to this, and it was simply accepted. It came to be the accepted view of the Church, and it was written into the canons of the Council of Trent:[106]

And since in this divine sacrifice which is performed in the Mass, that same Christ is contained in a bloodless sacrifice, who on the altar of the cross once offered himself with the shedding of his blood: the holy Synod teaches that this sacrifice is truly propitiatory, and through it it comes about that, if with true hearts and right faith, with fear and reverence, with contrition and penitence, we approach God we 'attain mercy and find grace to help in time of need' (Hebrews 4.16). For God propitiated by the oblation of this sacrifice, granting us grace and the gift of penitence, remits our faults and even our enormous sins. For there is one and the same victim, now offering through the ministry of the priesthood, who then offered himself on the cross; the only difference is in the method of offering. The fruits of this (the bloody) oblation are perceived more fully through the bloodless oblation; so far is it from taking any honour from the former. Wherefore it is rightly offered, in accordance with the tradition of the apostles, not only for the sins, penances and satisfactions and other necessities of the faithful living, but also for the dead in Christ, whose purification is not yet accomplished.

As it stands, this declaration seems to have many safeguards, with its stress on the necessity of faith and penitence and on the one sacrifice of Christ. But the abuses arose. The priest in whom there resided the power of consecrating the elements developed a unique authority. The idea of intention, the idea that the sacrament did that which it was intended to do, made it a means of salvation for a worshipper no matter what was in that worshipper's mind and heart. The insistence that the

[105] Gregory the Great, *Dialogue* 4.58, 59.
[106] Council of Trent (1545–1563), *Canons on the Holy Eucharist*, f, *On the Most Holy Sacrifice of the Mass*, chapter 2.

elements are the very substance of the body of Christ made them to be regarded with nothing short of an idolatrous reverence. If every celebration of the Mass is in fact a propitiatory act, then there is a very great possibility of multiplying masses, and the multiplication of them will inevitably in time lead to trading in them. The bringing of the dead into the orbit of propitiation begets the chantry system, by which endowments were given to ensure the saying of masses for the founder and the souls of his family. The idea – never officially recognized, but widely held – that the sacrifice on the Cross availed for original sin and that the sacrifice of the Mass availed for daily sins, deadly and venial alike, again made a traffic in Masses an extremely dangerous probability. A situation in which to all intents and purposes the sacrament becomes a propitiatory sacrifice to be made available by the priest is a situation which leads to perilous roads.

It was this situation which Luther attacked in his sermon on *The Babylonish Captivity of the Church*:

The third captivity of this sacrament is that most sacrilegious abuse by which it has come about that at this day there is nothing in the Church more generally received or more widely held than that the Mass is a good work and a sacrifice. This abuse has brought an endless flood of other abuses, until faith in the sacrament has been utterly extinguished and a divine sacrament has been turned into an article of trade, the subject of bargaining and business deals. Hence arise fellowships, fraternities, intercessions, merits, anniversaries, memorials; and such like pieces of business are bought and sold, and contracts and bargains are made about them. The entire maintenance of priests and monks depends on such things.

The doctrine of transubstantiation and the conception of the sacrament of the Lord's Supper as a propitiatory sacrifice were the two things which the Reformation denied and banished.

5

THE LORD'S SUPPER IN THE REFORMED CHURCHES

IT was inevitable that the Reformed Church should begin by expressing and defining its beliefs in contradistinction to the beliefs which it denied and repudiated.

We turn first to the Anglican position. John Cosin (1594–1672), the Bishop of Durham, wrote *A Letter to the Countess of Peterborough* in which he tabulated the differences between the Roman Catholic Church and the Church of England, together with the agreements. In regard to the sacrament of the Lord's Supper he tabulates three matters of disagreement:

That the priests offer up our Saviour in the Mass, as a real, proper and propitiatory sacrifice for the quick and the dead. . . .

That, in the Sacrament of the Eucharist, the whole substance of the bread is converted into the substance of Christ's body, and the whole substance of wine into his blood, so truly and properly, as that after consecration there is neither any bread nor wine remaining there; which they call transubstantiation. . . .

That there is a purgatory after this life, wherein the souls of the dead are punished, and from whence they are fetched out by the prayers and offerings of the living. . . .[1]

Here the three doctrines which are condemned are transubstantiation, the propitiatory sacrifice of the Mass, and the effectiveness of the Mass in shortening the period of souls in purgatory.

[1] The text of Cosin's Letter may be found in H. Bettenson, *Documents of the Christian Church*, pp. 427–432.

Lancelot Andrewes (1555–1626), Bishop of Winchester, in his *Responsio ad Apologiam Bellarmini* also denies the doctrine of transubstantiation, as a doctrine that no one ever heard of for the first four hundred years of the history of the Church, which came to light only in the last four hundred years before his own time. For him the presence of Christ in the sacrament was real. As to the method of the presence, 'we do not anxiously inquire, any more than how the Blood of Christ washes us in our baptism'. The power of the Word changes what was a mere element into a divine sacrament, but the substance remains as it was. The Eucharist is a memorial of the sacrifice of Christ, and may be called a commemorative sacrifice. 'Do you take away from the Mass your transubstantiation; and there will not long be any strife with us about the sacrifice. Willingly we allow that a memory of the sacrifice is made there. That your Christ made of bread is sacrificed there we will never allow.'[2]

Jeremy Taylor, Bishop of Down and Connor from 1661–1667, declares that since the Lord's Supper 'is a Commemoration and Representation of Christ's death, so it is a Commemorative Sacrifice'. He connects what happens on earth with what Christ still does in heaven. In heaven Christ ever makes intercession for us; there 'he offers still the same one perfect sacrifice'. Rather he represents it to God as 'finished and consummate'.

As Christ is a priest in heaven for ever and yet does not sacrifice himself afresh, nor yet without a sacrifice could he be a priest, but by a daily ministration and intercession represents his sacrifice to God and offers himself as sacrificed, so he does upon earth by the ministry of his servants.

By the prayers and in the sacrament he is represented to God as sacrificed. This is in effect at once a celebration of his death, and an applying of that sacrifice 'to the present and future necessities of the Church'.

It is ministerially and by application an instrument propitiatory;

[2] Stone, *History of the Doctrine of the Holy Eucharist*, 2.264–266; H. Bettenson, *Documents of the Christian Church*, pp. 433–435.

it is eucharistical; it is an homage and an act of adoration; it is impetratory, and obtains for us and for the whole Church all the benefits of the sacrifice, which is now celebrated and applied.

Here is the idea that in the sacrament Christ is not sacrificed again, but presented as already sacrificed, and in that presentation the forgiveness of God is found, through a sacrifice which was propitiatory when it was made, and is still propitiatory in its effects.[3]

The official Church of England position is in the Thirty-nine Articles, first composed in 1563, and in the revised form of 1571 accepted by the Upper and Lower Houses. The relevant articles are Articles 28 and 30:

The Supper of the Lord is not only a sign of the love that Christians ought to have among themselves one to another; but rather it is a Sacrament of our Redemption by Christ's death; in so much that to such as rightly, worthily, and with faith, receive the same, the Bread which we break is a partaking of the Body of Christ; and likewise the Cup of Blessing is a partaking of the Blood of Christ.

Transubstantiation (or the change of the substance of Bread and Wine) in the Supper of the Lord, cannot be proved by holy Writ; but it is repugnant to the plain words of Scripture, overthroweth the nature of a Sacrament, and hath given occasion to many superstitions.

The Body of Christ is given, taken, and eaten, in the Supper, only after an heavenly and spiritual manner. And the means whereby the Body of Christ is received and eaten in the Supper is Faith.

The Sacrament of the Lord's Supper was not by Christ's ordinance reserved, carried about, lifted up, or worshipped.

The Offering of Christ once made is that perfect redemption, propitiation, and satisfaction, for all the sins of the whole world, both original and actual; and there is none other satisfaction for sin, but that alone. Wherefore the sacrifices of Masses, in the which it was commonly said, that the Priest did offer Christ for the quick and the dead, to have remission of pain or guilt, were blasphemous fables, and dangerous deceits.

Out of this declaration many things have come. There has come the militant cry of J. C. Ryle (1816–1900), the Bishop of

[3] Jeremy Taylor, *The Great Exemplar* 3.15; H. Bettenson, *Documents of the Christian Church*, pp. 435–437.

Liverpool: 'There is a voice in the blood of the martyrs. What does that voice say? It cries aloud from Oxford, Smithfield and Gloucester. Resist to the death the Popish doctrine of the Real Presence under the forms of the consecrated bread and wine in the Lord's Supper!'[4] There has come the attitude of E. A. Knox, Bishop of Manchester (1847–1937), in his refusal to countenance any concession in the matter of vestments; 'It is impossible to dissociate in their minds (the evangelical Churchmen, so-called) the Eucharistic Vestments from the teaching that the Priest is a sacrificing Priest, offering upon the altar the memorial of the sacrifice of Calvary . . . . They will see in such permission a deliberate repudiation of the Book of Common Prayer as we now have it.'[5] Right at the other end of the scale is the famous or notorious *Tract XC*, the last of the *Tracts for the Times*, written by J. H. Newman in 1841. Its subject was *Remarks on Certain Passages in the Thirty-nine Articles*. Newman argued that it was transubstantiation that was condemned as a word rather than as a fact; and he argued that it was *Masses*, not *the Mass*, which were condemned. For to him the conversion of the elements and the sacrifice of the Mass were part of the doctrine of the Church, not simply of the Roman Catholic Church.[6]

What is probably the fairest and the best exposition of the view of the Church of England is in the *Responsio* of the Archbishops of England to the *Apostolicae curae* of Pope Leo XIII. Leo had attacked Church of England orders and sacraments, and the Archbishops reply. They deny that their Church regards the Lord's Supper as 'a bare commemoration of the sacrifice of the cross'. They also claim to teach the sacrifice of the Eucharist.

We observe . . . a perpetual memory of the precious death of Christ, who is himself our Advocate with the Father, and the pro-

[4] J. C. Ryle, *Light from Old Times*, p. 54; Quoted in M. L. Loane, *Makers of our Heritage*, pp. 34–35.
[5] E. A. Knox in a speech on a Resolution permitting the use of a white chasuble and alb; quoted in M. L. Loane, *Makers of our Heritage*, pp. 128, 129.
[6] The relevant parts of the Tract can be conveniently found in H. Bettenson. *Documents of the Christian Church*, pp. 448–453.

pitiation for our sins, according to his instruction, until his second coming. For, in the first place, we offer a 'sacrifice of prayer and thanksgiving', then we set forth and reproduce before the Father the Sacrifice of the cross, and through this sacrifice we 'obtain remission of sins and all other benefits' of the Lord's passion for 'all the whole Church'; finally we offer the sacrifice of ourselves to the Creator of all things, a sacrifice which we have already signified by the oblations of his creatures. The whole action in which the people has of necessity to take its part with the priest we are accustomed to call the Eucharistic Sacrifice. . . . But since it ought to be treated with extreme reverence, and to be regarded as a bond of Christian charity, not an occasion for subtle disputations, precise definitions of the manner of the sacrifice, and the principle by which the sacrifice of the eternal Priest is united with the sacrifice of the Church (which in some way certainly are one); these are in our judgment to be avoided rather than encouraged.[7]

This is a truly catholic view of the Lord's Supper. It is an act of thanksgiving. It is an act in which a sacrifice once and for all made is again presented to God and to man. It is an act of self-dedication. And legalistic definition, which is the begetter of differences, is deprecated in charity to all.

We now turn to the situation in the Church of Scotland. The General Assembly of 1647 adopted the Westminster Confession as the subordinate standard of the Church of Scotland, and it has remained so ever since. Hugh Watt claims that 'there never has been a sacramental controversy within the Church of Scotland or any of its branches'.[8] This may be so because of the clarity of the statement in the Westminster Confession. The statement is in chapter 29, and is entitled *Of the Lord's Supper*:

Our Lord Jesus the same night in which he was betrayed instituted the sacrament of his body and blood, called the Lord's Supper, to be observed in his church unto the end of the world, for the perpetual remembrance of the sacrifice of himself in his death, the sealing all benefits thereof unto true believers, their spiritual nourishment and

[7] Large sections of the *Responsio* are printed in H. Bettenson, *Documents of the Christian Church*, pp. 454–458.
[8] J. Hastings, *Encyclopaedia of Religion and Ethics*, vol. 5, p. 569, article on the Eucharist.

growth in him, their further engagement in and to all duties which they owe unto him, and to be a bond and pledge of their communion with him, and with each other, as members of his mystical body.

In this sacrament Christ is not offered up to his Father, nor any real sacrifice made at all for remission of the sins of the quick or dead; but only a commemoration of that one offering up of himself, by himself, upon the cross, once for all, and a spiritual oblation of all possible praise to God for the same; so that the Popish sacrifice of the mass, as they call it, is most abominably injurious to Christ's one only sacrifice, the alone propitiation for the sins of the elect.

The Lord Jesus hath in this ordinance appointed his ministers to declare his word of institution to the people, to pray, and bless the elements of bread and wine, and thereby to set them apart from a common to a holy use; and to take and break the bread, to take the cup, and (they communicating also themselves) to give both to the communicants, but to none who are not then present in the congregation.

Private masses, or receiving this sacrament by a priest, or any other, alone; as likewise the denial of the cup to the people; worshipping the elements, the lifting them up, or carrying them about for adoration, and reserving them for any pretended religious use; are all contrary to the nature of this sacrament, and to the institution of Christ.

The outward elements in this sacrament, duly set apart to the uses ordained by Christ, have such relation to him crucified, as that truly, yet sacramentally only, they are sometimes called by the name of the things they represent, to wit, the body and blood of Christ; albeit, in substance and nature, they still remain truly and only bread and wine, as they were before.

The doctrine which maintains a change of the substance of bread and wine into the substance of Christ's body and blood (commonly called Transubstantiation) by consecration of a priest, or by any other way, is repugnant not to Scripture alone, but even to common sense and reason; overthroweth the nature of the sacrament; and hath been and is the cause of manifold superstitions, yea, of gross idolatries.

Worthy receivers, outwardly partaking of the visible elements in this sacrament, do then also inwardly by faith, really and indeed, yet not carnally and corporally, but spiritually, receive and feed upon Christ crucified, and all benefits of his death; the body and blood of the Lord being then not corporally or carnally in, with, or under the bread and wine; yet as really, but spiritually, present to the faith of believers in that ordinance, as the elements themselves are to their outward senses.

The clarity and definiteness of this statement make it impossible for anyone who claims to receive it to believe in any kind of conversion of the elements or any kind of propitiatory sacrifice in the sacrament. It grounds everything in faith, and for faith the sacrament becomes an expression of gratitude for the past, an experience of the benefits wrought for us by Christ in his death, and a self-dedication for the future. Both in its denial of error and in its declaration of truth this declaration possesses an unmistakable clarity of thought and expression.

6

THE MEANING OF THE
LORD'S SUPPER FOR TODAY

The simple act of eating together has always been an expression of fellowship. The common meal was very much part of both of the backgrounds from which Christianity came. It was so in the Jewish way of life.

1. In the East, to admit a man to the table was always a sign of friendship. The Psalmist has it: 'Thou preparest a table before me in the presence of my enemies'.[1] The picture is that of a man fleeing across the desert with his enemies hot on his heels. He arrives at an encampment where the family are at a meal. He stands before the open tent in hesitation and in mute appeal. If the man in the tent stretches out his hand and offers him food, bread and salt, he is safe, for he will be accepted into the encampment and, if need be, defended to the last. But if the man in the tent turns away and refuses, the fugitive is left to face his enemies alone. The giving and the sharing of the meal is the mark of committed friendship. Those who sit at a meal are committed to each other, and committed to their host, and their host is committed to them.

2. In the East there was a regular custom of ratifying a treaty, or an agreement, or a covenant with a common meal. This is what Isaac and Abimelech, Jacob and Laban, David and Abner did.[2] After the covenant had been offered, accepted and made, it is said of the people: 'They beheld God, and ate and drank'.[3]

3. Part of the apocalyptic imagery of the last days was the

[1] Psalm 23.5.
[2] Genesis 26.30; Genesis 31.54; II Samuel 3.20.   [3] Exodus 24.11.

Messianic banquet which God would give to his people, when they would come from the north and the south, and the east and the west to be the guests of God in his kingdom.[4]

4. The custom of holding funeral feasts was widespread in the ancient world. We find reference to it in the Old Testament. In Jeremiah one of the grim things in a bleak future is that such a memory of the dead will not be possible. 'No one shall break bread for the mourner, to comfort him for the dead; nor shall any one give him the cup of consolation to drink for his father or his mother.'[5] In the time of sorrow one of the things that Ezekiel is forbidden to do is to eat the bread of mourners.[6]

These funeral feasts were carried over into the Christian Church, and often became a problem. Gregory of Nazianzen complained of the drunkenness at them.[7] Augustine speaks of the 'revelries and lavish repasts in cemeteries', and forbade them in AD 392, and says that all over they were abolished by the bishops.[8]

This is simply further proof that meals together were part of every occasion in ancient life.

5. In two particular forms of Judaism the common meal held a high place. It was an integral part of the Essene way of life.[9] For the Essene, every common meal of the community was a sacrament, to which he was admitted only after he had sworn 'a tremendous oath' of fidelity to God and to the community.[10] Josephus describes the Essene midday meal:

After the bath of purification they betake themselves to a dwelling of their own, into which no one of any other faith is allowed to enter. When they have cleansed themselves, they go into the refectory as into a sanctuary. After they have quietly taken their seats, the baker lays down the bread in order, and the cook sets before each a dish with a single kind of food. The priest prays before the meal,

---

[4] Cf. Luke 13.29.   [5] Jeremiah 16.7.   [6] Ezekiel 24.17.
[7] Gregory Nazianzen, *Orat.* 6.4 ff.; Chrysostom, *Homily 27 on I Corinthians 11*.
[8] Augustine, *Confessions* 6.2; *Letter* 22, *To Aurelius*, 4, 5, 6.
[9] For the Essenes in general see Josephus, *Antiquities* 15.10.4 f.; 18.1.5; *Wars of the Jews* 2.8.2-13; Philo, *Quod Omnis Probus Liber* 13-14; Pliny, *Natural History* 5.17.4; Eusebius, *Praeparatio Evangelii* 8.11.
[10] For the substance of the oath see Josephus, *Wars of the Jews* 2.8.2.

and none may eat before the prayer. After the meal he prays again. At the beginning and the end they honour God as the giver of food. Then they put off their garments as sacred and go back to work till evening, when they come again and eat in the same way.[11]

For the Essenes the fellowship meal was the centre of their community life.

The same was true of the Qumran Community. For them, too, the common meal was the centre of community life, and the sign of a man's reception into the community after a two-year preparation was his admission to the meal. There is a description of it in the document which Vermes calls *The Messianic Rule*.[12]

When they shall gather for the common table, to eat, and to drink new wine, when the common table shall be set for eating and the wine poured for drinking, let no man extend his hand over the first-fruits of the bread and wine before the Priest; for it is he who shall bless the first-fruits of bread and wine, and shall be the first to extend his hand over the bread. Thereafter the Messiah of Israel shall extend his hand over the bread, and all the congregation of the community shall utter a blessing, each man in the order of his dignity. It is according to this statute that they shall proceed at every meal at which at least ten men are gathered together.

It is clear that the common meal, sacramental in its conception, was very much the centre of the fellowship of the covenanters of Qumran.

6. Lastly, and most important of all, Jewish faith and devotion centred upon the Passover Meal, and it would be only natural that Jews, when they turned to Christianity, would take with them a custom and a tradition so deeply embedded in their lives.

We turn now to the way of life of the Greeks and the Romans. In their lives too the common meal was very much part of life.

1. In Greek life people were divided into *demes*, which were rather like tribes, and *phratriai*, which were rather like clans. When a man married a girl from another clan she had to

---

[11] Josephus, *Wars of the Jews*, 2.8.5.
[12] G. Vermes, *The Dead Sea Scrolls in English*, p. 121.

G

become a member of his clan, and the integrating into the new clan came at a clan meal. The clan meal signified the passing out of one family into another.

2. The *eranos* was a very common part of ancient life. It was what might be called a subscription meal. Trades and guilds and societies had these common fellowship meals.

3. Religious and sacramental meals were an essential part of ancient life.[13]

A great deal of what we would call private entertaining was done in temples. When a sacrifice was offered, it was seldom or never burned entire. Sometimes only a few hairs cut from the forehead of the victim were burned as a symbolic burning of the whole victim. The priests received part of the flesh of the victim as their right and perquisite. The worshipper also received part, and with his part he gave a feast to his friends in the temple precincts. So what we would call an invitation to dinner read like an invitation to dine with the god in whose temple the sacrifice was to be made and where the meal was to be held. Two second-century invitations read as follows:

Chaeremon invites you to dine at the table of the Lord Serapis, tomorrow fifteenth, at nine o'clock.[14]

Antonius, Ptolemaeus' son, invites you to dine with him at the table of the Lord Serapis, in the Serapaeum of Claudius, on the sixteenth, at nine o'clock.[15]

Even a social meal was a religious meal; even a dinner party was sacramental in character.

This goes back to a very primitive idea, and an idea not by any means extinct in New Testament times, in which the god was supposed to be not only a guest at the feast, but in some sense also the host, and in which he gave himself to his guests. The guests invite the god 'to the hearth as guest and host'. So in Rome at the *Iovis Epulum*, the banquet of Jupiter, Jupiter himself was invited to the table, with Juno and Minerva as fellow-guests.

The Mystery Religions all had their common meals. At

---

[13] S. Angus, *The Mystery-Religions and Christianity*, pp. 127–133.
[14] *Oxyrhynchus Papyri* 1.110.   [15] *Oxyrhynchus Papyri* 3.523.

Eleusis the sacrifice to Demeter and Korē was followed by a banquet in which the flesh of the victims was eaten. In the Mysteries of Mithra, bread and a cup of water were offered to the initiate. In the Samothracian Mysteries it was said that 'the priest shall break and offer the food, and pour out the cup to the initiates. In the Dionysus-Zagreus cult the communicants rushed madly upon the sacrificial animal, tore it to pieces, and ate it raw, believing that the god was resident in the offering.'[16] Angus says that these communal meals were in fact the main bond of brotherhood in the fellowship.[17] At them the initiate looked for communion with the god and nourishment for daily life.

The ancient world provides abundant examples of common meals wherein there were sought fellowship with some god, and fellowship of the worshippers.

This, then, is the Jewish and pagan background of the Christian meal of the Lord's Supper. When we turn to the Lord's Supper itself we find in it what we might call a series of movements.

1. There is the movement from the house to the Church. It is not in doubt that the Lord's Supper began as a family meal or a meal of friends in a private house. This was inevitable for the simple but sufficient reason that more than a century was to pass before there was such a thing as a church building. Christians were poor; still more important, Christianity was illegal. Its worship was therefore a thing of the house church and the small group and the home. It was there that the Lord's Supper was born in the Church. It was like the Jewish Passover which is a family festival and at which the father and the head of the household is the celebrant. There can be no two things more different than the celebration of the Lord's Supper in a Christian home in the first century and in a cathedral in the twentieth century. The things are so different that it is almost possible to say that they bear no relationship to each other whatsoever. The liturgical splendour of the twentieth century

[16] F. Cumont, *Religions Orientales dans le Paganisme Romain*, pp. 104, 174.
[17] S. Angus, *The Mystery-Religions and Christianity*, p. 131.

was in the first century not only unthought of; it was totally impossible. The Lord's Supper began in the house and moved to the Church.

2. The Lord's Supper moved from being a real meal into being a symbolic meal. The very way in which in the early accounts excesses of eating and drinking are condemned shows that it is a real meal which is in question. We have already noted that the Lord's Supper originated in a meal of hungry men, for the Jews who sat down to the Passover late in the evening had not eaten since at least midday. For many, for the slaves and the poor, the Lord's Supper must have been the one real meal of the week. The idea of a tiny piece of bread and sip of wine bears no relation at all to the Lord's Supper as it originally was. It was not until the Synod of Hippo in AD 393 that the idea of fasting communion emerged. The Lord's Supper was originally a family meal in a household of friends.

3. The Lord's Supper moved from bare simplicity to elaborate splendour.

Two passages may be set side by side. The first is from Tertullian's description of Baptism, and the description would apply equally to the Lord's Supper:

There is absolutely nothing which makes men's minds more obdurate than the simplicity of the divine works which are visible in the act, when compared with the grandeur which is promised thereto in the effect; so that from the very fact that with so great simplicity, without pomp, without any considerable novelty of preparation, finally without expense, a man is dipped in water, and, amid the utterances of some few words, is sprinkled and then rises again, not much the cleaner, the consequent attainment of eternity is esteemed more incredible. I am not a deceiver if, on the contrary, it is not from their circumstance, and preparation and expense that the solemnities of idols or the mysteries get their credit and are built up. O miserable incredulity which quite denies to God his own properties, simplicity and power![18]

The whole stress of this passage is on the bare simplicity of the Christian rite. With this stress on simplicity we may compare the words of Gregory of Nyssa a century later:

[18] Tertullian, *Concerning Baptism* 2.

Inasmuch as men when approaching emperors and potentates for the objects which they wish in some way to obtain from these rulers, do not bring to them their mere petition only, but employ every possible means to induce them to feel pity and favour towards themselves, clasping their knees, prostrating themselves on the ground, and putting forward to plead for their petition all sorts of signs to wake that pity, so it is that those who recognize the true Potentate, by whom all things in existence are controlled, when they are supplicating for that which they have at heart, some lowly in spirit because of pitiable conditions in this world, some with their thoughts lifted up because of their eternal mysterious hopes, seeing that they know not how to ask and that their humanity is not capable of displaying any reverence that can reach to the grandeur of that glory, they carry the ceremonial used in the case of men into the service of the Deity. And this is what worship is, that worship I mean which is offered for objects we have at heart along with supplication and humiliation.[19]

Here an elaborate worship is clearly contemplated.

This elaboration of worship and liturgy had certain moving causes.

1. The whole worship of the Church moved from the house to the church building as we have seen. That which had been a family occasion became a service at which the bishop dispensed the sacrament surrounded by the presbyters detached from the congregation. It inevitably became something to be watched almost at a distance.

2. The sacraments came to be exalted at the expense of preaching. It came to be felt that the dramatic picture of the sacrament was of more effect than the preaching of the word. In one sense it demanded less intelligence to look than to listen. The dramatic picture came to take the place of the reasoned account and appeal.

3. With the increasing idea of the conversion of the elements into the actual body and blood of the Lord, the sacrament became less and less the grateful memory of the death of Christ and more and more the awestricken encounter with the glorified King of heaven and of earth. It was coming into the presence

[19] Gregory of Nyssa, *On the Holy Spirit*. This and the previous passage from Tertullian are cited in A. V. G. Allen, *Christian Institutions*, in the chapter on the Lord's Supper, pp. 515–565.

of the King, and all the trappings of the court began to be used.

It is not difficult to see the immense gulf between the splendour of this magnificent liturgy and the vestments of the priests and the simplicity of the original meal in the Upper Room, and the original Lord's Supper in the Church in the house.

4. The Lord's Supper moved from being an act of the heart's devotion to being a centre of theological debate. It moved from being a dramatic and concrete picture into being an exercise in abstract and metaphysical thought. It began by simply confronting a man in dramatic and pictorial terms with the sacrifice of Jesus Christ. It began by saying quite simply, yet very vividly: 'Look what he did for you!' It ended with complicated questions of the real presence of Christ in the elements and of whether or not it was a propitiatory sacrifice, questions which in the early days it would never have occured to anyone even to ask.

5. The celebration of the Lord's Supper moved from being a lay function to a priestly function. In the New Testament itself there is no indication that it was the special privilege or duty of anyone to lead the worshipping fellowship in the Lord's Supper. In the *Didache* again there is no mention of any special celebrant. In fact the prophets are to be allowed to hold Eucharist as they will.[20] In Irenaeus the celebration is not assigned to any special person. In Justin Martyr the person who presides is the president of the brethren, and it is pointed out that the phrase so translated could quite legitimately be translated 'that one of the brethren who was presiding'.[21]

To all this there is one exception – Ignatius. In the Letters of Ignatius the bishop has acquired a place of paramount importance. 'We must regard the bishop as the Lord himself.'[22] Nothing must be done without the bishop and they must be subject to the bishop as to Jesus Christ.[23] They must follow the

[20] *Didache* 10.7.
[21] Justin Martyr, *First Apology* 65; cf. the translation of the passage and the footnote to it in the translation in the Ante-Nicene Library volume containing Justin Martyr and Athenagoras, p. 63.
[22] Ignatius, *To the Ephesians* 6.1.   [23] Ignatius, *To the Trallians* 2.1 f.

bishop, as Jesus Christ follows the Father.[24] 'It is good to know God and the bishop. He who honours the bishop has been honoured by God; he who does anything without the knowledge of the bishop is serving the devil.'[25] And, for our purposes, there is above all the instruction: 'Let that be considered a valid Eucharist which is celebrated by the bishop, or by one whom he appoints . . . It is not lawful either to baptize or to hold an *agapē* without the bishop.'[26]

The plain fact is that in this matter Ignatius stands alone. In the early period of the Church there is no other evidence that the celebration of the Eucharist was confined to any one person. But in Ignatius the celebration of the Eucharist has become the function of the ministry.

This situation is rendered more acute when there arises the view that it is by the act of consecration by the priest that the elements are converted into the body and blood of Jesus Christ. In Pope Leo XIII's epistle *Apostolicae curae*, in which he attacks the validity of Anglican orders, it is laid down that the special grace and power of the priesthood is 'the power of consecrating and offering the true body and blood of the Lord in that sacrifice which is no mere commemoration of the sacrifice accomplished on the cross'.[27] When the priest is credited with being the only person through whose action the consecration of the elements can take place, then the priest has a unique, unassailable and irreplaceable authority in the celebration of the sacrament. When the Church was the house Church, as it was in the beginning, as in the case of the Passover, so in the case of the Lord's Supper, it is entirely probable that it was the head of the household who presided at the sacrament.

No one is going to claim that the right to celebrate the sacrament should belong to anyone, irrespective of his character, of his devotion, of his instructedness, and of his training, so that all things may be done decently and in order. But there is no evidence from the earliest time that the celebration of the Eucharist was a priestly function, or an episcopal function.

---

[24] Ignatius, *To the Smyrnaeans* 8.1.   [25] Ignatius, ibid. 9.1.
[26] Ignatius, ibid. 8.1 f.
[27] H. Bettenson, *Documents of the Christian Church*, pp. 385 f.

The Church existed long before Ignatius. No doubt Ignatius came from a situation in which orthodoxy was in peril and heresy a menacing threat, but it is at least possible to argue that the Church took the wrong way when it took from the layman the right to celebrate the sacraments and confined it to either an ecclesiastical or a priestly class.

Whether the movement was in the right direction or not is something which we cannot at the moment lay down, but movement there was from the house to the Church, from real meal to symbolic meal, from simplicity to elaboration, from devotion to theology, from the concrete to the abstract, from the layman to the priest.

It is time now to return to the original meal in the Upper Room and to see what Jesus was trying to do at it. In our view we have in the New Testament records of the Last Supper, accounts, and reliable accounts, of an actual historical happening. We would not accept the view that what we have is an aetiological cult legend, formed and designed to provide a basis for a sacramental action which had largely come into the Church from its Hellenistic background. It seems to us that the very divergence in the accounts of the Last Supper are the best proof of that. If this had been a deliberately constructed cult legend, then we would have expected a stereotyped form – which is exactly what we do not get. The divergences are the proof that the roots of this are in history and not in liturgy.

We would begin with an assumption which we regard as basic. *In the last days of his life Jesus was consistently using dramatic prophetic action.* When the prophets met a situation in which it was difficult to get their message across, in which it was difficult to get people to see what they meant, in which people would neither listen nor understand, they turned their message into some vivid, significant action, as if to say: 'If you will not listen, you will look!' The prophets knew that eye-gate is often open when ear-gate is closed.

Ahijah wished to say that the kingdom was going to be split, and that ten tribes were going to secede with Jeroboam, and that only two were going to remain faithful to Rehoboam, the foolish king. So he dressed himself in a new robe. He then went out and met Jeroboam on the road. When he met him, he took his new robe and tore it into twelve pieces, and gave ten of them to Jeroboam and kept two. This, he said, was what was going to happen to the kingdom. Ten tribes would revolt to Jeroboam, and only two remain with Rehoboam.[28] People might not listen to words, but they would certainly stop to look at a prophet stripping himself of his robe in public and tearing it up. When Jeremiah wished to make the people see that subjection to Nebuchadnezzar was inevitable, he sent yokes and thongs to the neighbouring kings, and went about wearing a yoke on his own neck.[29] And when Hananiah the false prophet wished to indicate that Jeremiah, in his opinion, was mistaken, he went and removed the yokes from Jeremiah's neck and smashed them.[30] People might not listen but they were bound to see and to ask what all this was about. This was a method which Ezekiel continually used.[31]

We believe that in the last days Jesus continually used this method. The Triumphal Entry was a dramatic prophetic action claiming that he was King. The Cleansing of the Temple was a dramatic prophetic action claiming that he was Messiah. So the Last Supper was Jesus in dramatic prophetic action saying: 'Look! This is what they are going to do to me – but what is going to happen to me is for you!' In this Jesus was walking in the tradition of the prophets, and using this dramatic action to make men see what stated in words they refused to see and to understand.

This, then, will fix the meaning of his words. When we forget the layers of theological argument in which the Last Supper has been enwrapped, one thing stands out quite clearly. When Jesus said, 'This is my body', he was actually holding the bread in his hand. It was quite impossible that he was identifying his body and the bread, for his body was here and the bread was there. He can only have meant: 'This means, represents, my body.' When Luther wrote on the table: '*Hoc est corpus meum*', and when he thereupon insisted that the *is* necessarily asserted some kind of identity, he was asserting

<hr>

[28] I Kings 11.26–33. [29] Jeremiah 27.1–11. [30] Jeremiah 28.10 f.
[31] Ezekiel 4 and 5.

something that is just not true. In biblical language *is* frequently means *represents, stands for*. In the interpretation of the parable of the sower we read:

What was sown on rocky ground, this *is* he who hears the word, and immediately receives it with joy.

As for what was sown among the thorns, this *is* he who hears the word. . . .

As for what was sown on good soil, this *is* he. . . .[32]

In the interpretation of the parable of the tares we read:

The field *is* the world; the good seed *means* (so RSV; Greek, *is*) the sons of the kingdom; the weeds *are* the sons of the evil one; the enemy who sowed them *is* the devil; the harvest *is* the close of the age; the reapers *are* angels.[33]

In every one of these cases it is not in dispute that the word *is* means *represents, stands for, means*. This usage is completely natural and well authenticated. This, we believe, is what Jesus meant. We believe that Moffatt was completely right when he translated this: 'This means my body.' We believe that it still means this, and that the long discussions of wherein the identity of the bread and the body of Christ lies, and the whole paraphernalia of conversion and consecration are completely irrelevant. Something essentially simple and pictorial and crystal clear to the simplest mind has been turned into something obscure and in the end for simple people unintelligible and even magic.

When Jesus spoke in one form or another of the cup being the covenant in his blood, what he was saying is : 'This cup stands for the new relationship between man and God made possible at the cost of my death.' A covenant is a relationship between two people; the Greek *en* stands for the Hebrew *bᵉ*, which means *at the price of*.

Quite simply, the words of the sacrament are: 'This bread stands for my body which is going to be for you. This cup stands for the new relationship between man and God made

---

[32] Matthew 13.20, 22 f.   [33] Matthew 13.38 f.

possible by the death which I am going to die.' Here, in this vivid picture, as an ancient prophet might have done, Jesus told his men of his death and of what it meant.

Before we go on to ask what the sacrament of the Lord's Supper must mean to us, there is one other question at which we must look. If the Lord's Supper goes back to the Jewish Passover, and if Jesus took the Jewish Passover and remade it into the Lord's Supper, we have to ask why the Lord's Supper was not, like the Jewish Passover, an annual celebration. In our earliest account of it it is already weekly, for we read in the *Didache*: 'On the Day of the Lord come together, break bread, and hold Eucharist.'[34] On the face of it the same question applies to the Lord's Day. The Lord's Day is the memorial of the Resurrection of Jesus. It is because the Resurrection happened on it that the Sabbath, the last day of the week, was abandoned, and the Lord's Day, the first day of the week, adopted by the Christians as their sacred day. In the case of the Lord's Day the explanation is that in each Roman week there was a day called the Emperor's Day, and it was very natural for the Christians to have their Lord's Day. And what most likely happened was that the Lord's Day, so to speak, took the Lord's Supper with it, and the two became weekly together.

Let us now go on to see what the Lord's Supper ought to be for the Christian today.

1. It is the occasion of thanksgiving. The very word Eucharist means thanksgiving. Ignatius writes: 'Seek, then, to come together more frequently to give thanks (*eis eucharistian*) and glory to God.'[35] The first Eucharistic prayers, the prayers in the *Didache*, are almost entirely prayers of thanksgiving. There is first the prayer concerning the cup:

We give thanks to thee, our Father, for the Holy Vine of David, thy child, which thou didst make known to us through Jesus thy child; to thee be glory for ever.

There is the prayer concerning the bread:

We give thee thanks, our Father, for the life and knowledge which

[34] *Didache* 14.1.   [35] Ignatius, *To the Ephesians* 13.1.

thou didst make known to us through Jesus thy child; to thee be glory for ever.

There is the prayer 'after you are satisfied with food':

We give thanks to thee, O Holy Father, for thy Holy Name which thou didst make to tabernacle in our hearts, and for the knowledge and faith and immortality which thou didst make known to us through Jesus thy child; to thee be glory for ever. Thou, Lord Almighty, didst create all things for thy Name's sake, and didst give food and drink to men for their enjoyment, that they might give thanks to thee, but us hast thou blessed with spiritual food and drink and eternal light through thy child. Above all we give thee thanks that thou art mighty. To thee be glory for ever.[36]

The Eucharist is the time for thanksgiving to God for his gifts in creation and in redemption.

2. It is the demonstration of unity. Once again the prayers of the *Didache* stress this.

As this broken bread was scattered upon the mountains, but was brought together and became one, so let thy Church be gathered together from the ends of the earth into thy kingdom, for thine is the glory and the power through Jesus Christ for ever.

Remember, Lord, thy Church, to deliver it from all evil and to make it perfect in thy love, and gather it together in its holiness from the four winds to thy kingdom which thou hast prepared for it. For thine is the power and the glory for ever.[37]

This unity motif is evident in the Pauline passage which is generally called the warrant for the Lord's Supper, but it is concealed in the translation of the Authorized Version, which is based on an inferior text. The Authorized Version has:

He that eateth and drinketh unworthily eateth and drinketh damnation to himself, not discerning the Lord's body.[38]

In the same verse the Revised Standard Version has:

---

[36] *Didache* 9.1–3; 10.1–4.

[37] *Didache* 9.4; 10.5. The translations from the *Didache* are from the translation by Kirsopp Lake, *The Apostolic Fathers*, vol. 1, in the Loeb Classical Library.

[38] I Corinthians 11.29.

Anyone who eats and drinks without discerning the body eats and drinks judgment upon himself.

There is little doubt that the reading which the Revised Standard Version adopts is correct, and that *the Lord's* is not part of the original text. It is sufficient to say that the Chester Beatty papyrus manuscript of the Pauline Epistles, the first hand of Codex Sinaiticus, Codex Alexandrinus, Codex Vaticanus, and the first hand of Codex Ephraemi Rescriptus all omit these words. The correct phrase is 'without discerning the body'. The person condemned is not the person who does not discern that the elements he takes in his hands are the Lord's body. The person condemned is the person who does not discern that Christians are the Lord's body, and must be in unity before they dare approach the sacrament. The proof of this is the earlier part of the chapter. What is there condemned is the very fact that the Corinthian Christians, when they come to the sacrament, have divisions and factions through which all true fellowship is destroyed.[39] It is in fact these divisions and factions which have moved Paul to write about the Lord's Supper at all. The futher proof is that in the next chapter Paul goes on to write the famous passage about the Church as the body of Christ and the essential place of unity in it.[40] Paul's whole point is that to dare to partake of the sacrament while there are factions and sections and divisions in the Church, to dare to partake of the sacrament unaware or forgetful of the fact that we are a body and the body of Christ, is nothing less than a blasphemy. And this leaves us facing the terrifying fact that it may well be that so long as the Church is divided at the table of her Lord every celebration of the Lord's Supper is a crime against her Lord. The sacrament of the Lord's Supper ought to be the demonstration of unity, and – God forgive us! – it is in fact the centre of disunity. The only cure for this is to remember and never to forget that this table is the Lord's table, and not the table of any Church. At it we are the guests of the Lord Jesus Christ, not the guests of any part of his Church. No Church has any right to bar any man from a table which is

[39] I Corinthians 11.17–22.   [40] I Corinthians 12.14–30.

not hers, but her Lord's. This is not a private party; it is – or ought to be – a gathering of the guests of Jesus Christ. We have too long not discerned that we are all the body of Christ.

3. This sacrament is .a proclamation of the Gospel. Paul adds his own words to the close of the sacrament:

For,as often as you eat this bread and drink the cup, you proclaim the Lord's death until he come.[41]

The sacrament of the Lord's Supper is *kerygma* in its own right. Here in its vivid drama is the pictorial presentation of the facts of the Gospel. We may talk about the Word and the Sacraments, but this sacrament is the Word proclaimed in dramatic action. For that very reason we would hold that the sacrament of the Lord's Supper is almost always better left to itself without preaching, for the human words of any preacher can add nothing to, and may well often spoil, the heart-moving, soul-searching action of the sacrament.

4. This sacrament is the expression of Christian confidence. It proclaims the Lord's death *until he comes*. In the gospel version of it Jesus says that he will not drink again of the cup until he drinks it in his Father's kingdom.[42] Here in ringing tones there is expressed the eschatological hope of the Christian. It is not important how we interpret the idea of the Second Coming. What is important is that in the sacrament of the Lord's Supper we at one and the same time remember the past sacrifice of our Lord and affirm our certainty of his coming triumph. There is nothing in Christian worship which so looks to the past, the present and the future, as the sacrament of the Lord's Supper does.

5. There remain two things to say, and they are the most important of all. This sacrament is the sacrament of memory. It is a simple fact that in the New Testament the only definite instruction regarding the sacrament of the Lord's Supper is: 'Do this in remembrance of me'.[43] Here is the centre of the whole matter. First and foremost, we do this in order that we may remember Jesus Christ. It will be said by some at once

[41] I Corinthians 11.26.   [42] Matthew 26.29; Mark 14.25; Luke 22.17.
[43] I Corinthians 11.24.

that this is an inadequate view of this sacrament. But is it? Do we really realize what memory means? It is almost impossible to remember *simpliciter*. We always remember for some purpose or to some effect. Memory never operates in a vacuum. What then is the purpose and the effect of this sacramental memory? And why is it wrong to speak of 'a mere memorial'?

1. We remember to realize again what our blessed Lord has done and suffered for us. It is easy to forget. It is easy to lose the cutting-edge of emotion and realization. It is easy to forget that Jesus Christ suffered and died for us, and even when we remember, it is easy to remain unmoved. But in the sacrament, with its vivid picture, realization of what Jesus Christ did and suffered for us is rekindled and reborn.

2. This is to say that first we remember what Jesus Christ has done for us. The second step follows naturally. We remember in order once again to appropriate the benefits of Jesus Christ. We remember once again to receive. 'This is my body *for you*.' We need to receive again and again, for we sin again and again. In the sacrament we are confronted with the love of God in Jesus Christ, that we may take it to ourselves. There is the famous and oft-repeated tale of Rabbi Duncan, the famous Scots scholar and preacher. As he noticed a woman hesitating to take the cup, he said gently: 'Take it, woman. It was meant for sinners. It was meant for you.' In this act of memory we are not remembering either an heroic deed or a tragedy, and no more. We are remembering something done for us in order that we may appropriate it once again.

3. But there is something still more to be said. We have been speaking of remembering. But we are not remembering some one who is dead and gone, someone who lived and who died and who left a memory. We are not remembering someone whose place was in the past and who lives only in the pages of a history book. We are remembering someone who was crucified, dead and buried – *and who rose again*. We are remembering someone who is gloriously alive. And therefore we remember Jesus Christ in the sacrament in order to encounter Jesus Christ.

Here, O my Lord, I see thee face to face.

The memory turns into an experience and an encounter.

It is in this way that I would think of the real presence of Jesus Christ in the sacrament. The Risen Lord is universally present. He is not present in the sacrament any more than he is present anywhere else. As Brother Lawrence said, he felt as near to his Lord when he was washing the greasy dishes in the monastery kitchen as ever he did at the blessed sacrament. But what happens is that at the sacrament everything is done and designed *to make us aware* of that presence. He is not specially present, but we are made specially aware of his presence.

There is a power of places. It is long since my father and mother died, and there are times when I forget them, and even when I think of them the days seem very far away when they were here. But, if I go and stand beside a certain grave in a little highland cemetery, I can feel that, if I stretch out my hand, I will touch them. The sacrament of the Lord's Supper is not so much the place where we realize the real presence of our Lord, as the place where we realize the reality of the real presence of our Lord. The presence is not specially located in the bread and the wine, nor in the Church. It is a presence which is present always, everywhere. But the sacrament is the place where memory, realization, appropriation end in encounter, because we are compelled to become aware of him there.

Mere memory is a very misleading phrase. Memory always has a purpose, and, even if it has no purpose, it certainly has an effect. To remember, to realize, to appropriate, to encounter – this is what the sacrament of the Lord's Supper means to me.

4. All this must end in still another act on our part. It must end in renewed dedication. Here is where the other meaning of the word *sacramentum* must come in. It means a soldier's oath of loyalty to his Emperor, and that the sacrament must be for us too. As Arthur said of his knights:

> I made them lay their hands in mine
> And swear to reverence the king.

No experience such as we have described can end in anything other than a renewed pledge to the one whom we have encountered or experienced. It must surely be impossible to leave the sacramental table without a deeper devotion to the Blessed Lord whom we meet there.

We may end with the one fact which makes the Lord's Supper a permanent necessity in the Christian Church. T. C. Edwards in his commentary on I Corinthians makes the point. The Lord's Supper is the unchanging statement of that which is unchanging in Christianity. The centre of Christianity is what Jesus did. The Lord's Supper in its dramatic picture states that just as it is. Preaching talks about it; theology interprets it and conceptualizes it. The sacrament announces it. 'Ideas mark the progress, sacraments the fixity of Christianity. . . . Doctrines develop, sacraments continue, and help to anchor theological thought to its moorings. Paul does not hesitate to develop new truth, but he does not ever institute a new sacrament.' The Lord's Supper is the permanent dramatic pronouncement of the unchanging divine action in Jesus Christ, which theology interprets and reinterprets continuously.

H

ORDER FOR A
COMMUNION SERVICE

Jesus said:

> Blessed are the pure in heart for they shall see God.
> Eternal and ever-blessed God, so restrain every wandering thought and so banish every evil thought, that we this day being pure in heart may see you.

We remember how Jesus the Risen Lord was known to his friends in the breaking of bread; and how their hearts were set ablaze as they talked with him on the road.

> Lord Jesus, here in this chapel today, make yourself known to us in the breaking of bread, so that, having met you here, we may go from this place with hearts aflame with love of you.
>
> This we ask for your love's sake: Amen.

Praise

Prayer

If we tell God of our sin, we can depend on him in his goodness to forgive us. Let us ask forgiveness now.

> O God, our Father, there has been no part of this life of ours that has been fit for you to see.

In our homes

> We have been careless and inconsiderate;
> We have been moody and irritable and difficult to live with;
> We have treated those whom above all we ought to cherish with a discourtesy we would never dare to show to strangers;
>> For this forgive us, O God.

In this University and College

We have not been as diligent as we should have been;

We have been afraid to think, and to follow only truth;

We have not always borne each other's burdens and forgiven each other's faults;

Sometimes we have tried to offer to you and to men that which cost us nothing:

    For this forgive us, O God.

In the Church

We have found your service sometimes a burden and not a delight;

We have not always shown the love that brothers ought to show;

We have been so immersed in the details that we have sometimes lost the vision of the eternities;

We have often been too satisfied with self and too critical of others:

    For this forgive us, O God.

In life in the world

We have so often been careless in duty;

    slack in prayer;

    blind to the things which should have been our chief concern;

On us there has been so little of the love which is the magnet to draw men to you:

    For this forgive us, O God.

Let us be silent and in the silence let us make our own confession to God.

O God, our Father, we know that we are sinners, but we also know that we are forgiven sinners; help us here and now to accept the forgiveness and the absolution which you are offering to us.

And help us to prove our penitence and our gratitude by going from this place to live with something of the beauty of holiness and something of the loveliness of our Master upon us, so that men may know that we have been with Jesus.

Reading Lessons

Prayer

The Lord upholds all those who are falling and raises up those who are bowed down. Let us ask him for his help.
O God, bless us and help us today.
Those whose minds are perplexed, and who have more questions than they have answers;
Those who have temptations the power of which makes them afraid;
Those whose hearts are sore and whose eyes have known tears:
  Bless all such, O God.
Those for whom things are easy, that they may be kept from pride;
Those for whom things are difficult, that they be kept from discouragement and despair;
Those who are regretful for the past or afraid of the future:
  Bless all such, O God.
Bless any
  in anxiety of mind;
  in pain of body;
  in distress of heart.
Bless your Church in this country and throughout all the world; and so cleanse, purify and strengthen it that it may be a fit weapon for your purposes.
Bless our country, our Queen and our leaders, and in the days when decisions are difficult, guide them in the way that is right.
Bless this college and this university, and grant that those who teach and those who are taught may be one united band of brothers in you.
Bless those we love and those who are dear to us.

The Silence

From our deep darkness come we to your light;
From all our weakness to your peace and power;
And from our sinfulness to your great love;

Fulfil your promise and turn none of us away:
through Jesus Christ our Lord. Amen.

THE COMMUNION HYMN

Praise

The Grace of the Lord Jesus Christ be with you all

Let us hear how Paul tells how this sacrament began:
The tradition which I have passed on to you goes right back
to the Lord. That tradition tells that on the night on which
he was being delivered into the hands of his enemies, the
Lord Jesus took a loaf, and when he had thanked God for it,
he broke it and said:

This means my body which is for you.
You must continue to do this to make you remember me.
In the same way at the end of the meal he took the cup too,
and said:

This cup stands for the new relationship with God made
possible at the cost of my death.
You must continue to do this as often as you drink it to
make you remember me.

For every time you eat this loaf and drink this cup you are
publicly proclaiming the Lord's death until he comes again.

The Declaration of Faith

I come to the Lord's Table in obedience to the invitation and
command of Jesus Christ who suffered and died for me.

To him I owe the assurance that my sins are forgiven.
Through him I know that God is my heavenly Father.
On him alone I depend for grace to overcome all evil and to
do the right.
Within this fellowship and with all his followers I will strive
to maintain his honour upon earth.

As Jesus on the night on which he was betrayed took a common
loaf and a common cup of wine and used them to be signs of
truth eternal, I take this bread and this wine to be set apart
from their common use to this their sacred use this day.

O God, our Father, we know that you are always trying to speak to us in the common things and in the common experiences of life, and that in the midst of time you are always giving us glimpses of eternity. So let your Spirit be in us and be upon this bread and wine today that through them we may enter into our blessed Lord and he into us, that —

> they may tell us of his sacrifice;
> they may comfort us with his grace;
> they may confirm us in his strength;
> they may confront us with his love;
> they may fill us with his life.

As Jesus gave thanks so let us give thanks.

O God, our Father, we thank you for this sacrament.

> For all who down the centuries at this table have found the light that never fades;
> the joy that no man takes from them;
> the forgiveness of their sins;
> the love which is your love;
> the presence of their Lord:
> > We thank you.

> For all the means of grace:
> For the Church to be our mother in the faith;
> For your book to tell us of your ways with men;
> For the open door of prayer which you have ever set before us:
> > We thank you.

> For the memory of the unseen cloud of witnesses who compass us about;
> And for the presence still with us of those who are an inspiration:
> > We thank you.

> That you have made us as we are;
> For the dream that will not die;
> That somehow we cannot sin in peace;
> That even in the mud we are haunted by the stars:
> > We thank you, O God.

For Jesus Christ our blessed Lord:
> That he who knew no sin was made sin for us;
> that he came to seek and to save that which was lost;
> that he gave his life a ransom for many;
> that he was obedient even to death, the death of the
> cross;
> that having loved his own he loved them to the end:
>> We thank you.
> That he lived;
> that he died;
> that he rose again;
> that he is with us to the end of time and beyond; and
> that he is with us here today:
>> We thank you.

Bless the Lord, O my soul, and never forget what he has done for you; even so, Bless the Lord.

Hear this our thanksgiving through Jesus Christ our Lord. Amen.

The Invitation

Come, not because you are strong, but because you are weak.

Come, not because any goodness of your own gives you a right to come, but because you need mercy and help.

Come, because you love the Lord a little and would like to love him more.

Come, because he loved you and gave himself for you.

Lift up your hearts and minds above your cares and fears and let this bread and wine be to you the token and pledge of the grace of the Lord Jesus Christ, the love of God and the fellowship of the Spirit, all meant for you if you will receive them in humble faith.

I will take the cup of salvation and call upon the Lord.

Blessed are they who hunger and thirst after righteousness for they shall be filled.

O taste and see that God is good.

On the night on which he was being delivered into the hands of his enemies Jesus took a loaf, and when he had thanked God

for it, he broke it and said: this means my body which is for you. You must continue to do this to make you remember me.

So eat all you of it and so remember.

In the same way at the end of the meal he took the cup and said: This cup stands for the new relation with God made possible at the cost of my death. You must continue to do this as often as you drink it to make you remember me.

So drink all you of it and so remember.

Every time you eat this loaf and drink this cup you are publicly proclaiming the Lord's death until he comes again.

Let your light so shine before men that they may see your lovely deeds and give the glory to your Father who is in heaven.

Prayer

O God, our Father, send us from this place
    with the light of your hope in our eyes;
    and the fire of your love in our hearts.
Send us from this place
    conscious again of the unseen cloud of witnesses who
    compass us about;
    and certain of the presence of our blessed Lord.
Send us from this place
    sure of the forgiveness of sins
    and of the life eternal, to which there is no end.
Send us from this place
    sure that in this life you are with us
    and that afterwards you will receive us into glory.
[Bless all those who will do anything for you on Sunday.
    Give them such knowledge and love of yourself
    and such power and grace to tell of it
    that through them others also may come to know you
        and to love you.]

Our Father which art in heaven: hallowed be thy name; thy kingdom come; thy will be done in earth as it is in heaven. Give us this day our daily bread; and forgive us our debts as we forgive our debtors; and lead us not into temptation but deliver us from evil; for thine is the kingdom and the power and the glory for ever: Amen.

Praise

BIBLIOGRAPHY

A. V. G. Allen, *Christian Institutions*, 1898

S. Angus, *The Mystery-Religions and Christianity*, 1925
The Religious Quests of the Graeco-Roman World, 1929

Donald Baillie, *The Theology of the Sacraments*, 1957

Henry Bettenson, *Documents of the Christian Church* (World's Classics), 1943

J. G. Davies, *The Social Life of Early Christians*, 1954

James Hastings, *Encyclopedia of Religion and Ethics*, Vol. 5, 1912, Article 'Eucharist', pp. 540–570, by J. H. Srawley and Hugh Watt

A. J. B. Higgins, *The Lord's Supper in the New Testament*, 1952

J. Jeremias, *The Eucharistic Words of Jesus*, revised ed., 1966

D. Stone, *History of the Doctrine of the Holy Eucharist* (2 vols.), 1909

E. Underhill, *Man and the Supernatural*, 1927

INDEX OF BIBLICAL REFERENCES

INDEX OF NAMES

INDEX OF SUBJECTS